Spain Travel Guide

Explore the Country & Speak Spanish Like a Local!

3 Books in 1

Explore to Win

THIS COLLECTION INCLUDES THE FOLLOWING BOOKS:

Madrid Travel Guide

Barcelona Travel Guide

Valencia Travel Guide

BONUS: European Spanish Phrase Book

Table of Contents

$100+ FREE BONUSES

Spain Audio Pronunciations

Spain Travel Hacking Guide

Spain Travel Hacks Audiobook

Spain Visual Travel Guide

Spain Travel Itineraries

Spain Budget Travel Guide

Scan QR code to claim your bonuses

— OR —

visit bit.ly/451ZoyA

BOOK 1

Madrid Travel Guide

Explore to Win

Introduction

Ever craved a comforting dish of home-style spaghetti, only to be delightfully surprised by the rich, bold flavors of an unexpected seafood paella? Well, imagine that unexpected delight being an entire city full of surprises at every turn. Welcome to Madrid, where the mundane is rare, and every street corner reveals a new spectacle!

Let's be honest; we've all been there, right? When we think we've got a city figured out from those travel brochures, only to land there and realize that reality is an entirely different world. The bustling plazas, the sparkling monuments, the bubbling tapas bars— it's all too overwhelming and too amazing to be contained within the confines of a brochure.

That's where this book comes in. It is your knowledgeable tour guide, reliable companion, and delightful entertainer, all in one. It navigates you through the charming labyrinth of Madrid, ensuring a continuous stream of excitement.

So, what can you expect from this colorful adventure of a journey? If you think Madrid is just another run-of-the-mill city with a couple of museums, a famous football team, and a few tapas bars here and there, prepare to have your expectations shattered, and in the best way possible!

Madrid is a city of layers, with centuries of history, culture, and tradition woven into its fabric. As you peel back each layer, you'll discover a new facet of this mesmerizing metropolis. Perhaps it'll be the grandeur of the Royal Palace, the creativity bursting from every corner of Malasaña, the tranquility of the El Retiro Park, or the tantalizing aromas wafting from a food market in Salamanca.

And then there are the people – the Madrileños – whose infectious zest for life is as intoxicating as a glass of chilled sangria on a hot summer's day. Through this book, you won't just visit Madrid; you'll live it! You'll feel the heartbeat of the city, resonate with its rhythm, dance to its melody, and leave with a piece of Madrid forever imprinted on your soul.

But it's not just about the sights, sounds, and flavors. This guide is also about making you feel comfortable and confident as you navigate through Madrid. You'll learn essential Spanish phrases to help you haggle at the markets, order your meals, ask for directions, and maybe even make a few local friends!

From the historical wonders of Plaza Mayor to the artistic marvels of the Prado Museum, this book will navigate you through it all. And while we're at it, we'll also dive into Madrid's vibrant culinary scene. Imagine savoring a mouthwatering cocido madrileño at a local taberna or feasting on the world's best churros at San Gines – this guide will make those experiences a reality for you!

You, my friend, are holding the key to Madrid – the pulsating heart of Spain – created by 'Explore to Win'. We're not just authors; we're Madrid-obsessed enthusiasts who've spent years exploring every nook and cranny of this colorful city. Living, loving, and learning about Madrid, we've gathered insider knowledge and experiences, and we can't wait to share them with you!

We've stumbled out of flamenco bars at dawn, doused in the infectious laughter of locals. We've locked horns with shrewd vendors at the El Rastro flea market, all for that one elusive trinket. We've stood, frozen in awe, before the relentless raw emotion of Picasso's Guernica. And, trust us, we've hollered our lungs out in the euphoric frenzy of a Santiago Bernabéu Stadium match. What we mean to say is that we've fully soaked up the Madrileño life – and now it's your turn.

Think of this guide as our little love letter to Madrid – brimming with insider info and pro tips, all served with a side of saucy banter. We want you to visit Madrid and truly connect with it, feel its pulse, and maybe even fall head over heels for it, just like we did.

So, here's the plan: You strap in, we lead the way. Together, we embark on a roller-coaster journey, exploring Madrid's fascinating history, culture, and charisma. The grand reveal begins with Chapter 1: Madrid – A Journey Through Time and Culture, where we'll witness the city's evolution from a humble Moorish town to the dynamic metropolis it is today. Ready to dive in? ¡Vamos! Madrid awaits, and trust us, by the end, you won't just be a tourist – you'll be a Madrileño at heart. Let's roll!

Chapter 1: Madrid – A Journey Through Time and Culture

"Madrid is the most Spanish of all cities, the best to live in, the finest to drink in."
-Hemingway

Just imagine, if cities were people, Madrid would be that eccentric yet charming uncle at family gatherings. The one with a seemingly never-ending collection of wild tales and life stories, each more fascinating than the last. He's been around the block a few times, had his share of highs and lows, seen it all, and lived to tell the tales. Yet, he's still young at heart, always up for a good time, and full of infectious energy that can light up even the dreariest days.

Madrid is a grand old city that refuses to grow old. It's a historical metropolis that seamlessly marries its vibrant past with an ever-evolving present. In other words, Madrid is a history book where the pages are constantly rewritten.

And just when you think you've seen all that Madrid has to offer, the city surprises you with yet another gem. Maybe it's a hidden garden in the middle of the city, a secluded tapas bar where the locals hang out, or a secret street art spot that transforms a dull wall into a vibrant canvas. Madrid is the gift that keeps on giving.

So, buckle up, hold onto your hats (and your sangrias), and get ready for a ride through Madrid's history, culture, and gastronomy. By the end of this chapter, you'll have a newfound appreciation for this grand old city that's young at heart.

Historical Background and Cultural Significance of Madrid

Let's roll back the reel a bit, shall we? Madrid's saga begins around the ninth century, when a certain Emir Muhammad I, thought it would be a smashing idea to build a defensive fortress overlooking the Manzanares River. Like the proud parent of a Lego masterpiece, little did he know that this humble castle would one day become the nucleus of a bustling metropolis.

Fast forward a few centuries, and Madrid finds itself playing host to Spanish royalty. King Philip II, probably looking for a change of scenery, moved his court to Madrid in the 16th century, effectively making it the capital of Spain. Madrid must have felt like the shy kid who's suddenly elected prom king!

From then on, Madrid was caught up in a whirlwind of transformations, like a caterpillar in a particularly busy chrysalis. Royal palaces sprung up, grand squares were designed, and magnificent boulevards took shape, each adding another pearl to Madrid's growing necklace of wonders.

But history's not always about the glitz and glam, is it? Madrid's seen its share of dark days too. It's been under siege, it's been invaded, it's witnessed revolts, and it's lived through dictatorships. But just like a Flamenco dancer in the face of a stormy applause, Madrid faced every challenge head-on, never losing its spirit.

Now, what about culture, you ask? Well, imagine if culture were a delicious pot of stew, Madrid would be the one that's been simmering for centuries, absorbing flavors from every era, every ruler, and every migrant who's called this city home. It's a melting pot of influences from the Moors, the Christians, the Gypsies, and, more recently, from immigrants across Europe, Africa, and South America.

This cultural medley reflects everything from Madrid's architecture, where Gothic cathedrals rub shoulders with Moorish fortresses, to its music and dance, where Flamenco riffs blend with modern rock beats.

And who can forget the fiestas? Madrid loves a good party. The city celebrates everything from saints and seasons to food and art. If there's one thing you'll learn about Madrid, it's that any excuse is a good excuse for a fiesta!

So, there you have it, a tour through Madrid's rich historical tapestry and cultural cauldron. But remember, we've only just scraped the surface. There's so much more to uncover, so many more stories waiting to be told.

Local Traditions and Festivals: A Madrileño Party Parade

If you ever think that your calendar is chock-full, wait until you peek at a Madrileño's planner. The residents of Madrid have a knack for finding celebration in every nook and cranny of the calendar, turning ordinary days into extraordinary fiestas. If there were an Olympic medal for partying, Madrid would probably be doing a victory lap right now.

Let's start with Three Kings Day in January, Madrid's answer to Christmas. Dream of this: a bright parade of floats, musicians, and, yes, three kings who throw candies to the crowd. It's like Mardi Gras met Santa Claus and decided to throw a party in Madrid.

Then we've got San Isidro in May, where Madrileños dress in traditional attire and head to the Pradera to dance, eat, and drink in honor of their patron saint. It's a bit like stepping into a time machine and getting off at a 19th-century country fair.

And then there's the Fiesta de la Paloma in August, a colorful street party complete with live music, traditional dances, and everyone dressed in chulapos and chulapas. It's a real hootenanny, Madrileño-style!

This is just a sneak peek of Madrid's fiesta fever. There are plenty more where these came from, each with its own unique flavor, rhythm, and spirit. It's a bit like being on a merry-go-round of festivities that never stops turning!

Madrid's Architecture: From Hapsburg Havens to Soaring Skyscrapers

If architecture were a language, Madrid would be a linguistic genius fluent in countless dialects. The cityscape is a veritable dialogue between different architectural styles, each contributing to Madrid's unique skyline.

Let's start our architectural journey in Hapsburg Madrid, shall we? There are cobblestone lanes, plazas lined with cafes, and charming old buildings whispering tales of yore. Plaza Mayor, a grand square with symmetrical red brick buildings and the Casa de la Panaderia, is like the living room of this old Madrid, where people gather to chat, eat, and watch the world go by.

Next up, we step into the elegance of the Bourbon era, embodied in the grand boulevards and imposing buildings around the Paseo del Prado. Madrid's 'Golden Triangle of Art,' home to the Prado, Reina Sofia, and Thyssen museums, is like the crown jewels of this era.

But Madrid's architectural marvels aren't just about the past. Fast forward to the 21st century, and you've got audacious skyscrapers and avant-garde buildings pushing the envelope of architectural design. The Cuatro Torres Business Area, with its futuristic skyscrapers, is like Madrid's postcard to the future.

So, whether you're a history buff, a design enthusiast, or just someone who appreciates a good-looking building, Madrid's architecture is bound to leave you awe-struck. It's like walking through a living museum where every building has a story to tell. Buckle up, folks, because our architectural adventure is only just beginning!

Madrid Unplugged: The Local Lowdown

Ever danced with a churro at midnight? Ever woken up from a midday siesta to the sound of flamenco heels tapping away in the distance? Ever witnessed the sun-drenched streets transform into a playground of the moon? In Madrid, where the clock ticks a little differently, and the ordinary becomes extraordinary.

The Great Tapas Tango: When the sun bows out, and the moon takes center stage, Madrileños step out for a dance. A dance with tapas! The 'tapeo' is more than just a culinary crawl; it's a tantalizing tango with an array of Spanish bites that gets your taste buds twirling in joy.

Siesta-ville: Just when the afternoon sun is at its dramatic best, Madrid decides to take a theatrical pause. Siesta isn't merely an afternoon nap here; it's an act of communal peacefulness, a collective curtain call before the grand evening performance begins.

Twilight and Tunes: Forget the clichéd "the city never sleeps." In Madrid, the city really "wakes up" at night. Think of a daily festival of sounds, colors, and tastes that makes New Year's Eve look like a dress rehearsal.

The Artful Dodgers: Madrid is an art installation in constant evolution. From the revered Prado Museum to the spray-can wizards decorating the streets, every corner of Madrid is a frame waiting to capture your amazement.

The Beautiful Game: In Madrid, football is more than just a game; it's a religion. A passionate sermon delivered on a grassy altar, cheered by a sea of believers in Real Madrid or Atletico jerseys. You don't just watch a match here; you participate in a high-stakes ritual of joy, despair, and exhilaration.

Fiesta Fandango: If there's one thing Madrid knows, it's how to throw a fiesta. Whether it's the elaborate San Isidro or the summer-long Veranos de la Villa, each event is a vibrant dance where tradition twirls in the arms of revelry.

Now, this is your ticket to the Madrid Fiesta. But remember, this city doesn't unfurl itself on paper. It's a sensory symphony best experienced in person - through the clink of sangria glasses, the taste of sizzling tapas, the echoing laughter in its plazas, and the passionate spirit of its people.

Madrid's Daily Life

Okay, hold my paella, we're about to navigate through the spectrum of Madrid's daily life. Let's stitch together the fabric of Madrid, detail by detail.

The Coffee Chronicles: If caffeine were a song, Madrid would be its album. From corner cafes serving piping hot café con leche to hipster coffee shops brewing cold press from single-origin beans. It's like sipping a world tour from your demitasse!

Markets and Mercados: Madrid's markets are like treasure chests brimming with fresh produce, seafood, and delicacies. Navigate El Rastro's labyrinth of stalls or wander through Mercado de San Miguel's gastronomic wonderland. It's like playing a real-life game of 'taste and seek'!

Tapas Tasting Tour: Madrid is a tapas lover's dream. From patatas bravas in bustling La Latina to delectable seafood pintxos in chic Salamanca, the city is a sprawling tapas tableau. It's like the city is playing culinary jazz and each tapa is a vibrant note!

Street Art Stroll: Madrid's graffiti artists paint the town red, and blue, and green... Embark on a street art safari in edgy Lavapiés or trendy Malasaña. It's like Madrid's walls have enrolled in art school, and boy, are they acing their classes!

Vamos a la Playa: Who said you need a coast to build a beach? In Madrid, beach bars spring up faster than you can say "mojito". It's like the city decided, "Who needs the sea? We'll make our own waves!"

Flamenco 101: The pulsating beats of Flamenco are Madrid's heartbeat. Venture into a tablaos for a passionate performance that'll make your heart race and feet tap. It's like signing up for a drama, dance, and music masterclass, all rolled into one intense performance!

The Late-Night Life: When the sun sets, Madrid dawns its party hat. From rooftop lounges with skyline views to basement clubs thumping with techno, Madrid's nightlife is as varied as a box of churros – long, sweet, and deep-fried in fun!

Parks and Recreation: Madrid's parks are like urban jungles - only with less jungle and more manicured lawns, elegant fountains, and picturesque pavilions. Whether it's rowing in Retiro's lake or picnicking in Casa de Campo, there's a park for every whim and fancy.

Fashion Forward: Madrid is a catwalk disguised as a city. Trendy boutiques, vintage stores, and high-end brands rub shoulders along its stylish streets. Whether you're a high-street junkie or a thrift-shop hopper, Madrid's got you covered – quite literally!

Neighborhood Narratives: Madrid is like a patchwork quilt, with each neighborhood adding its unique pattern. From Chueca's LGBTQ+ vibrancy to Chamberí's old-world charm, every barrio tells a different tale.

Day Trip Diary: Need a break from Madrid's hustle? The city has a Rolodex of picturesque towns and historical cities on speed dial. A tour of Toledo's medieval alleys or Segovia's Roman aqueduct is just a short trip away. It's like Madrid has friends in high (and far) places!

Art for Art's Sake: Madrid's art scene is like a bottomless jar of Nutella – rich, satisfying, and you just can't get enough! Go beyond the Prado and explore contemporary art at CaixaForum or immerse yourself in the surreal world of Dalí at Reina Sofia.

Madrid for Families: Madrid might be a late-night reveler, but it knows how to keep kids entertained. From puppet shows in Retiro to interactive exhibits at Museo de Ciencias Naturales, Madrid is like a giant playground that doesn't believe in bedtimes.

Unusual Madrid: Peel off Madrid's touristy veneer and discover its quirks. Visit an ancient Egyptian temple, explore Europe's largest urban street art mural, or enjoy a sunset at a secret rooftop bar. It's like going on a treasure hunt where X marks the unusual!

The Santiago Bernabéu and Wanda Metropolitano Stadiums: Welcome to the hallowed grounds of football worship. Take a pilgrimage to these iconic stadiums and experience the passion, drama, and nail-biting thrill of a live match. It's like a heart-stopping telenovela but with goals instead of plot twists!

Key Takeaways

- Madrid is a vibrant city with a rich history and a unique culture that beautifully blends the old with the new.

- From the royal Hapsburg Madrid to the modern skyscrapers, Madrid's architecture is a reflection of its ever-evolving identity.

- Madrileños know how to throw a party! Madrid's calendar is chock-full of local traditions and colorful festivals.

- Madrid's unique rhythm is best captured in its local customs, be it the tapas tango, siesta-ville, or the beautiful game of football.

- Whether it's the local markets, parks, coffee culture, or nightlife, there's always something happening in Madrid to pique your interest.

Action Steps:

- ✓ Deepen your understanding of Madrid by researching more about the places and traditions mentioned in this chapter.

✓ Start a Madrid bucket list. Write down the experiences you want to have, foods you want to try, and places you want to visit.

✓ Start learning a few basic Spanish phrases that will come in handy when you visit.

Alright, my dear fellow wander luster, we've danced our way through the beating heart of Madrid in this chapter. You've been an excellent partner on this whirlwind waltz through history, culture, fiestas, and everything that makes Madrid tick. But don't catch your breath just yet. Our adventures have only just begun.

So, grab that map, lace up those exploring boots, and get ready to embark on an all-access tour of Madrid's iconic attractions in Chapter 2. Madrid's not done with you yet, amigo!

Chapter 2: Madrid's Attractions

'Here is a city built in a wilderness. Philip II chose the site for no other reason than that it was the geographic center of Spain.'
– Gerald Brenan

Ever find yourself lost in a supermarket, trying to choose the right jam from a bewildering array of options? Well, get ready for a similar sensation, because Madrid is like a colossal supermarket of sights, each attraction more enticing than the other. A royal palace here, a world-class museum there, and oh look, a magnificent park right around the corner! Now, wouldn't it be a pickle to choose? But fret not, for we've got your back. Let's dive headfirst into the delightful labyrinth of Madrid's star attractions.

Landmarks and Museums

Inside the Royal Palace

Drama. Grandeur. Splendor. And, no, we're not talking about the latest season of a popular TV series. Welcome to the Royal Palace of Madrid! If walls could talk, these ones would probably be sporting a Spanish accent, whispering tales of gallant kings, beautiful queens, mischievous court jesters, and probably the odd ghost or two.

As the largest functioning royal palace in Europe, this place is not just big; it's 'where's-the-map-I'm-lost' big. With over 3,000 rooms filled with priceless art, gilded furniture, and luxurious tapestries, you'll feel like you've stepped into an episode of Lifestyles of the Rich and Royal.

A stroll through the palace is like a crash course in 'how to live like a royal.' The Throne Room, with its extravagant decorations and a ceiling that would make the Sistine Chapel blush, is a sure-fire jaw-dropper.

Don't miss the Royal Armoury, where you can imagine suiting up for battle with suits of armor, shields, and weapons that have seen more action than a Hollywood blockbuster.

And just when you think you've seen it all, the palace gardens, Campo del Moro, welcome you with a green oasis that is the perfect antidote to the palace's opulent interiors. Think carefully manicured lawns, beautifully sculpted fountains, and an atmosphere that whispers, "Sit down, relax, and bask in the royal ambiance."

Practical Info:

Location: Right at the heart of Madrid, within a short walk from Opera Metro Station (Lines 2 and 5). City buses (Lines: 3, 25, 39, and 148) also service the area.
Tickets: Basic fare is €12 for visitors who do not qualify for a reduced or free rate. Reduced fare is €6 for citizens between the ages of 5 and 16 (ID or passport required for ages 14 to 16), seniors over 65, and students up to age 25 with a current national or international student card. Check the official website for the most updated information.

Hours: Open on weekdays from 10 AM to 7 PM, and on Sundays from 10 AM to 4 PM.

Tips & Tricks: Arrive early to beat the crowds, and consider a guided tour for a more in-depth understanding of the palace's history. Don't miss the stunning views from the Sabatini Gardens!

Safety: Security checks are in place at the entrance. Sharp objects, large bags, and backpacks are not permitted inside the palace.

Accessibility: The palace is fully wheelchair accessible, with lifts and adapted restrooms. Service animals are allowed for visitors with disabilities.

Plaza Mayor: Madrid's Living Room

Plaza Mayor is Madrid's living room, a grand square where the city's life unfolds. Whether it's Christmas markets, street performances, or simply people enjoying a cup of coffee in the surrounding cafes, there's always something happening. The square's history is palpable in its architecture, from the fresco-laden Casa de la Panadería to the statue of King Philip III.

Practical Info:

Location: Plaza Mayor, 28012 Madrid, Spain

Tickets: Free

Hours: Always open

Tips & Tricks: Try the calamari sandwich from one of the surrounding cafes, it's a Madrid specialty.

Accessibility: The plaza is fully accessible for wheelchair users.

Safety: As with all popular tourist areas, keep an eye on your belongings.

The Almudena Cathedral

The Almudena Cathedral, with its unique blend of architectural styles, holds an enchanting tale of Madrid's historical evolution. The construction of the cathedral had a very turbulent timeline, with its initiation in 1883 followed by decades of halts due to economic constraints and the Spanish Civil War. When its doors finally opened to the public in 1993, the cathedral presented a captivating fusion of Gothic revival and modern neoclassical styles that had evolved over its century-long construction. Its younger age compared to other European cathedrals gives it a freshness that is as vibrant and welcoming as the city of Madrid itself.

Practical Info:

Location: Calle de Bailén, 10, 28013 Madrid, Spain.

Tickets: Free access to the cathedral, museum, and rooftop visit at 6 €.

Hours: Open every day from 9 AM to 8:30 PM.

Tips & Tricks: Climb the rooftop for panoramic city views.

Accessibility: Fully wheelchair accessible.

The Green Lung of Madrid: Retiro Park

Once upon a time, in the landlocked city of Madrid, there was a green oasis called Retiro Park. A haven for everyone from love-struck poets, Tai Chi masters, and street performers to ducks that think they rule the roost. This sprawling urban paradise is home to more than 15,000 trees, with each leaf whispering a different tale. There's a grand lake too where rowboats bob around like clumsy dancers, and the owners probably won't charge you if you bring your own pirate flag.

Art? Culture? They're hidden in every corner, like a city-wide game of hide and seek. Be it contemplating the dramatic "Fallen Angel" statue, or becoming part of the audience at a spontaneous puppet show, Retiro Park is your perfect retreat from Madrid's urban bullfight!

Practical Info:

Location: Plaza de la Independencia, 7, 28001 Madrid, Spain.

Tickets: Entrance to the park is free, but bring some change for the ice cream vendors.

Hours: Open year-round. From October to April: 6 AM-10 PM, May to September: 6 AM-midnight.

Tips & Tricks: Beware of the Chess Grandpas! They look innocent, but they play a mean game.

Accessibility: Smooth paths and plentiful benches make this park wheelchair and nap-friendly. Even the ducks have their own ramps.

Prado Museum

Ever wondered what Mona Lisa's cousin might look like? Or how Picasso would paint your pet turtle? You'll find answers to questions you never knew you had in the labyrinth of artistry that is the Prado Museum. Housing one of the finest collections of European art, the Prado is an art lover's delight and a historian's playground. Here, every painting tells a story, every sculpture sparks a conversation, and every artistic period punches you right in the feels. It's like walking into a time machine designed by a star-studded team of artists from across the ages. Be prepared to lose track of time, and don't worry if you walk out talking in iambic pentameter – it happens to the best of us.

Practical Info:

Location: Calle de Ruiz de Alarcón 23, Madrid, Spain.

Tickets: General admission is 15€. Under 18s, over 65s, and students up to 25 years of age get in for 7.5€. There are free-entry times, but it's best to check online because those slots are like the golden snitch of the Prado Quidditch.

Hours: Monday to Saturday: 10 AM – 8 PM. Sunday and holidays: 10 AM – 7 PM.

Tips & Tricks: Bring a snack or a significant other, because you might find yourself lost in Goya's dark universe or El Greco's surreal realms for longer than you anticipate.

Accessibility: The museum is fully accessible, with wheelchairs and walking frames available. Make sure to ask for the audio guide specifically created for visitors with visual impairments.

Reina Sofia Museum

Have you ever looked at a square and thought, "This could be a bit more... abstract"? If so, welcome to the Reina Sofia Museum! It's the place where Picasso's 'Guernica' hangs out, and where Dali's dreamscapes come to life. The museum is a cornucopia of modern and contemporary art that pushes boundaries, raises questions, and occasionally makes you go, "huh?" But isn't that what art's all about? It's a ride on the wild side of human creativity where the surreal meets the sublime, and where your brain cells get a serious workout. Just remember, there are no wrong answers in the Reina Sofia. But there may be a few floating apples.

Practical Info:

Location: Calle de Santa Isabel, 52, Madrid, Spain.

Tickets: The standard ticket is 12€. Concession tickets are 5€, and under 18s, over 65s, and unemployed individuals get in for free. For an extra workout, consider taking the stairs.

Hours: Monday to Saturday (except Tuesday): 10 AM - 9 PM. Sunday: 10 AM - 2:30 PM.

Tips & Tricks: Try to keep a straight face when you say, "Yes, I see the existential crisis in this brushstroke" - it makes the whole experience more fun.

Accessibility: The museum is fully accessible and provides visual aids, tactile models, sign language guides, and wheelchairs on demand. There's even a guide dog called Salvador Doodle, but he's usually off-duty.

Thyssen-Bornemisza Museum:

Ever wish you could time travel through seven centuries of art in a single afternoon? The Thyssen-Bornemisza Museum has got your back. From medieval masterpieces to avant-garde adventures, it's like binge-watching your favorite art history series but without the commercials. Expect to rub shoulders with Rembrandt, Van Gogh, Degas, and Kandinsky, as you navigate this vast visual extravaganza. If your eyes are popping out from sheer aesthetic delight, don't worry - that's a normal reaction. And remember, when in doubt, always blame it on the Impressionists.

Practical Info:

Location: Paseo del Prado, 8, Madrid, Spain.

Tickets: General admission is 13€, while reduced tickets are 9€ for pensioners and students. As for kids under 12 and unemployed folks, the art feast is on the house.

Hours: Tuesday to Sunday: 10 AM - 7 PM. Monday: Closed (Even art needs a day off).

Tips & Tricks: Wear comfortable shoes; time travel can be rough on the soles. And bring a notebook - you never know when you might be inspired to sketch your own masterpiece.

Accessibility: The museum is wheelchair-friendly, offers a touch tour for the visually impaired, and has induction loops for the hearing impaired. It's like the Justice League of museums - everyone's included!

Santiago Bernabéu Stadium: The Temple of Football

Welcome to the Santiago Bernabéu Stadium, where legends are born and dreams come true. This isn't just a football stadium; it's a cathedral of sporting passion, home to the mighty Real Madrid and the stage for countless memorable football moments. Whether you're a die-hard fan or a casual observer, stepping onto the Bernabéu's hallowed grounds is like stepping into a vortex of pure, unadulterated footballing excitement.

Practical Info:

Location: Av. de Concha Espina, 1, 28036 Madrid, Spain

Tickets: Ticket prices start at 25 € and can go up depending on the match. Guided stadium tours are also available.

Hours: Tours operate Monday to Saturday 9:30 AM – 7:00 PM, Sundays and Holidays 10:00 AM – 6:30 PM. Matchday hours vary.

Tips & Tricks: Book your tickets online to avoid long queues.

Accessibility: The stadium is fully accessible, with wheelchair seating and lift access.

Safety: The stadium area is usually crowded and bustling, particularly on match days, so keep an eye on your belongings.

Puerta del Sol: The Beating Heart of Madrid

If Madrid were a body, the Puerta del Sol would be its beating heart. This bustling square, one of the busiest places in Madrid, is a hub of activity. This is where the locals gather for New Year's Eve celebrations, where protests happen, and where tourists start their journey. It's where you'll find the famous Bear and the Strawberry Tree statue, Madrid's symbol. In short, Puerta del Sol is where it's all happening.

Practical Info:

Location: Plaza de la Puerta del Sol, s/n, 28013 Madrid, Spain

Tickets: Free

Hours: Always open

Tips & Tricks: Look out for the plaque marking "Kilometer Zero," the geographical center of Spain.

Accessibility: Being a flat and spacious public square, it is wheelchair friendly.

Safety: It's usually busy but always maintain awareness of your belongings due to the high traffic of people.

Casa de Campo: Madrid's Royal Retreat

Bigger than Central Park and packed with more adventures than a box set of Indiana Jones, welcome to Casa de Campo, the emerald jewel in Madrid's crown. It's a forest of fun that has it all - picnic spots, a zoo, an amusement park, and even a lake for boating! One minute you're mingling with the meerkats, the next you're screaming on the roller coaster, and then quietly meditating on a tranquil boat ride. Casa de Campo is Madrid's Disneyland, Animal Kingdom, and SeaWorld rolled into one, but with less commercialization and more authentic charm.

Practical Info:

Location: Paseo de la Puerta del Ángel, 1, 28011 Madrid, Spain

Hours: Open 24/7. However, individual attractions like the zoo or amusement park may have different opening times.

Tickets: Free entrance to the park. Individual attractions have their own ticket prices.

Tips & Tricks: Bring comfortable shoes, the park is huge! Also, bring a picnic if you want to save on food.

Accessibility: Wheelchair accessible paths are available.

Safety: Generally safe, but as with all parks, be aware of your surroundings.

Madrid Rio: Riverside Rendezvous

Just when you thought Madrid had shown all its cards, it pulls out the ace - Madrid Rio. This rejuvenated riverfront park is where the Madrileños escape the urban jungle for a slice of riverside heaven. Joggers, cyclists, skateboarders, and picnic-goers - everyone finds their sanctuary here. And the views? Spectacular! Madrid Rio is the perfect selfie spot with the royal palace, Almudena Cathedral, and the Segovia Bridge as the backdrop. It's Madrid's version of London's Thames Path or New York's Hudson River Greenway, but with more sangria spots.

Practical Info:

Location: Paseo de la Virgen del Puerto, s/n, 28005 Madrid, Spain

Hours: Open 24/7

Tickets: Free entrance

Tips & Tricks: Don't forget to bring your camera or smartphone for some amazing pictures.

Accessibility: The paths are mostly flat and are accessible for wheelchairs.

Safety: Well-lit paths and plenty of people around make this a safe area even after dark.

El Rastro Market: The Flea Market Where Every Item Tells a Story

Welcome to El Rastro, Madrid's legendary flea market! It's more than just a market; it's a thrilling treasure hunt in the heart of the city. As you wander through the bustling stalls, you'll come across everything from vintage clothes and antique furniture to quirky knick-knacks and charming curiosities. Who knows what treasures you might stumble upon?

Practical Info:

Location: Plaza de Cascorro and Ribera de Curtidores, between Ronda de Toledo and Embajadores

Tickets: Free

Hours: Every Sunday and public holidays, 9 AM - 3 PM

Tips & Tricks: Arrive early for the best finds and don't forget to haggle!

Accessibility: The market is in a pedestrian area but can get crowded.

Safety: As it gets crowded, keep an eye on your belongings.

Gran Via: The Spanish Broadway

Gran Via is Madrid's bustling main artery, a lively and vibrant avenue brimming with shops, restaurants, and iconic buildings. Often dubbed as the 'Spanish Broadway', Gran Via is a hub of entertainment and is home to Madrid's vibrant theater scene. With its impressive early-

20th-century architecture and the energetic pulse of city life, a stroll down Gran Via is an experience in itself.

Practical Info:

Location: Gran Via, Madrid, Spain

Tickets: Free

Hours: Always open

Tips & Tricks: Don't miss the Telefónica Building, an emblem of Gran Via's unique architecture.

Accessibility: The sidewalk is broad and well-maintained, making it easily accessible.

Safety: The area is generally safe but can be crowded, so keep an eye on your belongings.

Templo de Debod: An Ancient Egyptian Temple in the Heart of Madrid

The Templo de Debod is a slice of ancient Egypt right in Madrid. It's a genuine, 2,200-year-old Egyptian temple that was gifted to Spain in 1968. Today, it stands as a stunning testament to ancient Egyptian architecture and offers some of the best views of the Madrid sunset.

Practical Info:

Location: Calle Ferraz, 1, 28008 Madrid, Spain

Tickets: Free

Hours: Tuesday to Friday, 10 AM – 2 PM and 6 PM – 8 PM; Saturday and Sunday, 10 AM – 2 PM; closed on Mondays.

Tips & Tricks: Visit at sunset for a spectacular view.

Accessibility: There's an elevator at the entrance for wheelchair users.

Safety: The area is well-lit and safe.

Cibeles Palace and Fountain: A Symbol of Madrid

Cibeles Palace, with its impressive architecture and majestic fountain, is one of Madrid's most iconic landmarks. It's a beloved symbol of the city and a popular gathering spot for locals. Whether you're admiring the grandeur of the palace or making a wish at the fountain, Cibeles is a must-visit spot on your Madrid adventure.

Practical Info:

Location: Plaza de Cibeles, 28014 Madrid, Spain
Tickets: Palace visits are free, but certain exhibitions may have a fee.
Hours: Palace: Monday to Sunday, 10 AM - 8 PM. Fountain: always accessible.
Tips & Tricks: Don't miss the palace's viewpoint for a panoramic view of Madrid.
Accessibility: The palace is accessible, with ramps and elevators.
Safety: The area is well-lit and usually busy, making it safe for tourists.

Off the Beaten Path: Madrid's Hidden Gems

A city isn't just about its famous landmarks, world-class museums, or bustling squares. It's also about the little alleys, hidden courtyards, and unassuming locales that hold a world of secrets. Welcome to the offbeat heart of Madrid, where the city's soul truly resides.

Matadero Madrid: An Artistic Resurrection of the Slaughterhouse

How do you transform a slaughterhouse into a hotspot of culture and creativity? Welcome to Matadero Madrid! Here, every nook and cranny oozes creativity, as if the building itself swallowed a rainbow and a Picasso for breakfast. A cornerstone of Madrid's cultural scene, Matadero hosts exhibitions, performances, workshops, and even an outdoor cinema. So, if you've ever wondered what it's like to watch a movie in a former slaughterhouse, now's your chance. Let's just say it's... 'a cut above' the rest!

Practical Info:

Location: Paseo de la Chopera, 14, Madrid, Spain.
Tickets: Entry to the Matadero is free. So is the air of creative inspiration. Breathe it in!
Hours: Tuesday to Friday: 4 PM - 10 PM. Weekends: 11 AM - 10 PM. Monday: Closed (the creativity beast needs to rest too).
Tips & Tricks: Pack a sketchbook or a journal. The raw, industrial charm of Matadero is highly contagious for sparking creativity.
Accessibility: The Matadero is fully wheelchair accessible. Its avant-garde spirit is accessible to all!

Mercado de Motores: Vintage Treasure Trove

Imagine if a train station decided to throw a garage sale. Welcome to Mercado de Motores! Once a month, the old Delicias Train Station transforms into a bustling vintage market where local designers, antique dealers, and second-hand sellers convene. It's like a trip down memory lane on a steam engine, complete with retro tunes, food trucks, and old-world charm. If you're hunting for a vinyl record, a vintage poster, or a dress that screams the 1960s, hop aboard this nostalgia express. And remember, one person's 'junk' is another person's treasure!

Practical Info:

Location: Museo del Ferrocarril, Paseo de las Delicias, 61, Madrid, Spain.
Tickets: Free entry!
Hours: Second weekend of each month, Saturday and Sunday: 11 AM - 10 PM.
Tips & Tricks: Keep an open mind and let your curiosity lead. This isn't just a shopping spree; it's an adventure into the past.
Accessibility: The market is wheelchair accessible. All aboard the inclusion express!

Key Takeaways

- **Santiago Bernabéu Stadium:** A must-visit for sports enthusiasts. The home ground of Real Madrid offers thrilling matches and a peek into football history.
- **Puerta del Sol:** This bustling square is the literal heart of Madrid and Spain. Don't forget to take a picture with the Bear and the Strawberry Tree statue.
- **Plaza Mayor:** Steeped in history, the Plaza Mayor offers a spectacular setting for food, events, and people-watching.
- **El Rastro Market:** A treasure trove where you can haggle and hunt for unique antiques, art, and knick-knacks every Sunday and public holiday.
- **Gran Via:** Madrid's vibrant main artery, bustling with shops, restaurants, and theaters. Don't forget to admire the early-20th-century architecture.

- **Templo de Debod:** An authentic piece of ancient Egypt right in Madrid's heart, offering beautiful views of the sunset.
- **Cibeles Palace and Fountain:** One of Madrid's most iconic landmarks, beloved by locals and visitors alike. Be sure to check out the panoramic view from the palace's viewpoint.
- **Madrid Rio:** A rejuvenated riverside park that's perfect for a leisurely walk, bike ride, or picnic.
- **Casa de Campo:** Madrid's largest park, offering a range of activities, from boating to zoo visits.
- **Mercado de Motores:** This monthly market is a paradise for vintage lovers and bargain hunters.
- **Matadero Madrid:** An avant-garde cultural center that hosts a variety of events and exhibitions.
- **Thyssen-Bornemisza Museum:** The home of an eclectic and globally significant art collection.
- **Reina Sofia Museum:** A must-visit for modern art lovers. It houses Picasso's Guernica, among other significant works.
- **Prado Museum:** Spain's main national art museum, featuring one of the world's finest collections of European art.
- **Retiro Park:** A green oasis in the heart of the city, perfect for boating, leisurely walks, or just relaxing by the lake.
- **The Almudena Cathedral:** A beautiful blend of architectural styles that stands as a symbol of Madrid's resilience.
- **The Royal Palace:** A grand monument to the Spanish monarchy. The interior tour is well worth it.

Action Steps

✓ Plan Your Route: With so many places to visit, it can be overwhelming. Plot out your journey on a map to ensure you're making the most of your time in the city.

✓ Be a Smart Packer: Madrid's weather can be a bit unpredictable. Pack layers, comfy shoes for those cobbled streets, and maybe an umbrella, just in case.

✓ Set Up Alerts: With so much happening in Madrid, you don't want to miss out. Set up alerts or join local online forums to stay in the loop about events during your visit.

Remember, Madrid isn't just a destination; it's an experience. Dive deep, explore its nooks and crannies, and let the city surprise you. ¡Hasta luego! Your Madrid memories are just waiting to be made.

Chapter 3: Living La Vida Madrileña: Diving into Madrid's Heartbeat

"Adventure is worthwhile in itself."
- Amelia Earhart

Ever wondered what makes Madrid's heart tick? Why, when midnight strikes, the city is buzzing more than a coffee-addict on a Monday morning? Or why a simple meal in Madrid can feel like an Oscar-winning performance? Well, amigo, you're about to unravel the city's mysteries beyond the postcard-perfect sights.

In this chapter, we're turning the volume up to 11, going off-script, and dancing to Madrid's very own symphony. From the unsung lullabies of its dawn to the roaring anthems at midnight, we'll synchronize our steps to Madrid's pulsating beat. Ready to tango?

Madrid's Culinary Scene: From Tapas to Tortillas!

The pleasure of Madrid on a plate! You might've heard, "We are what we eat." Well, in Madrid, you'll become a delightful mix of history, passion, and sunshine with every bite. Let's plunge fork-first into dishes exclusive to Madrid and the best joints to sample them. And for my plant-powered amigos, worry not, we've got the vegetarian/vegan spins on these classics lined up too!

Cocido Madrileño

Where the meat-lovers rejoice!

About: A hearty stew that Madrid folks swear by during colder days. Made from chickpeas, veggies, and a generous mix of meats.
Location: La Bola – a traditional taberna located at Calle de la Bola.
How to Get There: Hop on the Metro Line 3 and stop at Ventura Rodriguez.
Veg/Vegan Twist: Many traditional spots now offer a meatless version with tofu or seitan. Ask for "Cocido Madrileño Vegetariano".

Bocadillo de Calamares

Madrid in a sandwich.

About: Golden, crispy squid rings served in a baguette. Simple yet oh-so-delicious.
Location: Casa Rúa – a haven for squid sandwich aficionados on Calle Ciudad Rodrigo.
How to Get There: It's a short walk from the Puerta del Sol Metro station.
Veg/Vegan Twist: Some joints offer battered vegan alternatives made from king oyster mushrooms!

Oreja a la Plancha

For the brave-hearted!

About: Grilled pig's ear, crispy on the outside, gelatinous inside. A delicacy!
Location: Taberna El Almendro, tucked away in the La Latina neighborhood.
How to Get There: Metro Line 5 to La Latina.
Veg/Vegan Twist: Look for "setas a la plancha" instead, grilled mushrooms offering a similar texture.

Churros con Chocolate

Sweet dreams are made of these.

About: Golden churros to dunk in a cup of thick, velvety chocolate.
Location: San Ginés Chocolatería on Pasadizo de San Ginés.
How to Get There: A stone's throw away from Sol or Ópera metro stations.
Veg/Vegan Twist: Churros are typically vegan! Just ensure the chocolate doesn't contain dairy.

Rosquillas de San Isidro

Festive munchies.

About: Soft or crispy anise-flavored donuts, famously consumed during the San Isidro festivities.
Location: Any local bakery during May, especially in the San Isidro area.
How to Get There: Metro Line 5 to Marqués de Vadillo.
Veg/Vegan Twist: Vegan bakeries in Madrid offer these with plant-based ingredients.

Sopa de Ajo (Garlic Soup)

A bowl of warmth!

About: A humble soup made with garlic, old bread, paprika, and sometimes an egg cracked on top. It's rustic comfort in a bowl.
Location: El Sur de Huertas in the Barrio de las Letras.
How to Get There: Metro Line 1 to Antón Martín.
Veg/Vegan Twist: Usually vegetarian. For a vegan version, skip the egg.

Huevos Rotos

Broken eggs for a whole heart!

About: Fried potatoes with over-easy eggs on top. Rip them apart and let the yolk ooze!
Location: Casa Lucio on Calle de la Cava Baja.
How to Get There: Metro Line 5 to La Latina.
Veg/Vegan Twist: Ask for tofu or vegan scramble instead of traditional eggs.

Torrijas

Spain's answer to French Toast.

About: Bread soaked in milk or wine, fried, and sweetened with honey or sugar. A Holy Week classic!
Location: La Antigua Pastelería del Pozo on Calle del Pozo.
How to Get There: Metro Line 3 to Sol.
Veg/Vegan Twist: Look out for versions using almond or oat milk in vegan-friendly bakeries.

Tips & Tricks:

- Lunchtime (2-4 PM) is sacred. Expect a bustling atmosphere.
- Locals typically dine late. 9 PM dinners are the norm.
- Always check if the restaurant offers a 'menu del día'. It's a daily set menu, often at a steal!
- Don't shy away from asking for vegetarian/vegan alternatives. Madrid's culinary scene is evolving!
- Madrid is a tapeo culture. 'Tapeo' is hopping from one tapas bar to another. So, be adventurous. If one spot tickles your fancy with a particular dish, another one right around the corner might surprise you with something even more delightful.

- If you're trying to fit into the Madrileño vibe, enjoy your meals leisurely. No rush. It's as much about the food as it is about the experience, conversations, and soaking in the ambiance.
- Many small businesses still honor the traditional siesta. Between 2 pm to 5 pm, you might find that some establishments, especially in non-touristy areas, shut their doors. It's a wonderful time to relax in a park or café.
- In many traditional bars in Madrid, you'll get a free tapa with each drink you order. Seek out older establishments, especially outside the city center.
- Tap water in Madrid is delicious and perfectly safe to drink. Save money and the environment – ask for 'agua del grifo' (tap water) when eating out.

Nightlife and Madrid's Late Nights

Why Do Madrileños Dine Late?

To understand Madrid, you must first get your internal clock in sync with its tempo. Madrileños are night owls, and there are historical, cultural, and even geographical reasons for this.

Historical Roots: The Spanish Civil War and the subsequent dictatorship disrupted the country's traditional schedules. The regime wanted to align its working hours with the rest of mainland Europe, even though Spain, geographically, aligns better with the UK's time zone. The mismatch between natural and social time means the sun sets later, pushing everything back.

Cultural Significance: Socializing is an integral part of Spanish culture. Whether it's the 'sobremesa' chat after meals or the evening 'paseo' (stroll), taking the time to be with family and friends is paramount. The longer evenings allow more social hours after work.

The Siesta Factor: The tradition of siesta creates a bifurcated workday, leading to later finishing times and, subsequently, later dinnertimes.

Making the Most of Madrid's Nightlife

1. Start with Tapas: Before the party starts, head to a local 'taverna' for tapas. These bite-sized delights are more than just food; they're a social activity. La Latina is a favorite area for traditional tapas hopping.

2. Flamenco Fusion: The passionate art of Flamenco isn't just preserved in tourist shows. Head to places like 'Casa Patas' or 'Las Carboneras' for an authentic experience or visit more modern spots blending Flamenco with Jazz and Rock.

3. Rooftop Revel: Madrid's skyline is dotted with rooftop bars offering mesmerizing views. 'Círculo de Bellas Artes' and 'The Hat' are among the top spots to sip on a cocktail under the stars.

4. Dance the Night Away: From pulsating electronic beats at 'Mondo Disko' to indie rock vibes at 'Ochoymedio', Madrid has a vibrant club scene that caters to all tastes.

5. Night Markets and Late-night Eateries: Markets like 'Mercado de San Ildefonso' or 'Platea' transform into buzzing gastronomic hubs in the evening, combining gourmet food with live entertainment.

6. Cultural Nightcaps: Some museums, including the Reina Sofia, occasionally open their doors for nighttime visits and events. A unique way to experience art!

7. Chillout Zones: If you're not in the mood to dance, places like 'El Estudio' offer a cozy environment to relax, listen to live music, and enjoy a drink.

Madrid Nightlife Venues

Casa Patas

- **Location:** Calle de los Cañizares, 10.
- **Getting There:** Metro station Sol or Tirso de Molina.
- **Best Time:** Shows typically start around 10:30 PM, but get there by 10 PM to secure a good spot.
- **What to Look Out For:** It's an authentic Flamenco experience. Don't miss their signature drinks and regional tapas.
- **Tips & Tricks:** Book in advance, especially during the weekends. It fills up quickly!

Círculo de Bellas Artes Rooftop Bar

- **Location:** Calle de Alcalá, 42.
- **Getting There:** Metro station Banco de España.
- **Best Time:** Sunset for a mesmerizing view, but anytime post 8 PM offers a buzzing atmosphere.
- **What to Look Out For:** The panoramic view of Madrid, especially the Gran Vía.
- **Tips & Tricks:** It can get windy up there, so carry a light jacket. Also, there's an entry fee which includes a drink.

Mondo Disko

- **Location:** Calle de la Duquesa, 9.

- **Getting There:** Metro station Noviciado.
- **Best Time:** After 1 AM, when the crowd starts pouring in.
- **What to Look Out For:** Their lineup of international DJs.
- **Tips & Tricks:** It's more of an electronic music crowd, so wear comfy shoes for dancing!

Mercado de San Ildefonso

- **Location:** Calle de Fuencarral, 57.
- **Getting There:** Metro station Tribunal.
- **Best Time:** Evening hours, starting 7 PM, when the food stalls start their gastronomic magic.
- **What to Look Out For:** Variety of tapas and gourmet delights from various regions of Spain.
- **Tips & Tricks**: Be adventurous with your food choices. It's a place to explore regional Spanish cuisines!

El Estudio

- **Location:** Calle de Echegaray, 3.
- **Getting There:** Metro station Sol or Sevilla.
- **Best Time:** Anytime from 9 PM onwards.
- **What to Look Out For:** Its intimate atmosphere is perfect for a laid-back evening.
- **Tips & Tricks:** They often have live jazz or acoustic sessions, so keep an eye out for their schedule.

Safety Tips for Night Owls in Madrid:

- **Watch Your Belongings:** As with any energetic city, be wary of pickpockets, especially in crowded areas or when using public transport late at night.

- **Limit Alcohol Consumption:** Enjoy responsibly and always watch your drink.
- **Use Licensed Taxis:** If traveling back late and not using public transport, ensure you're getting into a licensed taxi.
- **Stay Informed:** Before heading to any venue, check its latest reviews on platforms like TripAdvisor for recent experiences of fellow travelers.
- **Keep Emergency Numbers Handy:** The general emergency number in Spain is 112.
- **Trust Your Instincts:** If a place or situation feels off, trust your gut and stay safe.

Enjoying Madrid's nightlife is about immersing yourself in its vibrant energy while being smart and safe. The city is waiting for you to explore its nocturnal heartbeat. ¡A disfrutar!

Festive Fever – Madrid's Lesser-Known Traditions You Simply Can't Miss

If there's one thing that'll make you adore Madrid even more, it's the city's lesser-known festivals. Think of it this way: while everyone's busy watching the mainstream movie, we'll be in that indie theater next door, getting a genuine, quirky experience.

Fiesta de la Trashumancia:

Where? Throughout the city center.
When? Usually, the end of October.

Sheep in Madrid? Yep, you heard that right! Every year, herds of sheep are driven right through the city center, echoing the ancient rights of shepherds to migrate their flocks. This is a throwback to the 13th-century Spanish tradition. Plus, for vegetarians and vegans, no sheep are harmed during this parade; it's just a nod to history!

How to Get There: Just hang around the city center, especially near Cibeles, and you'll hear them before you see them.

Local's Tip: Be sure to wear comfy shoes; you might want to join the parade!

Fiesta de San Cayetano:

Where? Rastro and Lavapiés neighborhood.
When? Early August.

Madrid's Rastro district comes alive with colorful street decorations, traditional dress, and music. This is a warm-up act for San Isidro, and is much less crowded.

How to Get There: Take Metro Line 3 and get off at Embajadores or Lavapiés.

Local's Tip: Don't forget to taste the limonada (it's not what you think - it's a mix of wine, soda, and chopped fruit) that's traditionally served. But hey, ask if it's vegan or not; sometimes they sneak in a dash of spirits derived from animal products.

Noche de los Teatros:

Where? Various theaters around the city.
When? Usually in March.

A celebration of Madrid's theatrical scene, on this night, theaters throw open their doors with free or heavily discounted performances.

How to Get There: Depends on the theater, but many are around Gran Via, easily accessible by Metro.

Local's Tip: Some popular ones might get crowded. So, be early or go for the smaller, quirkier venues for a truly local experience.

Fiesta de la Almudena:

Where? Around the Cathedral and the Royal Palace.
When? November 9th.

This is the feast of Madrid's patron saint. While it's religious at heart, it's full of concerts, activities, and of course, churros!

How to Get There: Metro Line 5 to Opera Station.

Local's Tip: Check out the impressive floral offerings at the statue of the Virgen de la Almudena.

Madrid's Shopping Secrets – Beyond the Usual Suspects!

If you're tired of those typical touristy spots (I'm side-eyeing you, El Rastro), then I've got a treat in store for you. Literally. Madrid's local markets are a kaleidoscope of colors, tastes, and, most importantly, deals!

Let's don those comfy shoes, grab a reusable shopping bag (Mother Earth says thanks!), and venture where the savvy locals shop.

Mercado de la Paz:

Where? Located in the heart of Salamanca district.

What? A mix of gourmet eats, fresh produce, and some lovely wine spots.

How to Get There: A quick walk from the Retiro Park. Metro: Serrano or Velázquez stations.

Local's Tip: Keep an eye out for the small artisanal cheese stands. Vegan? Ask for vegan cheese; some stands have begun stocking them!

Mercado de San Fernando:

Where? The bustling district of Lavapiés.
What? A global market echoing the diversity of the neighborhood. Think Moroccan spices next to Japanese sushi stalls!

How to Get There: Metro Line 3 to Lavapiés station.

Local's Tip: On weekends, local artists display their crafts in the central area. Great for unique souvenirs!

Antón Martín Market:

Where? Central Madrid, not far from Atocha station.
What? Traditional stalls mixed with hipster organic juice bars and vegan eateries.

How to Get There: Short walk from Puerta del Sol. Metro: Antón Martín station.

Local's Tip: Dive into the basement! There's a mini-cinema showing indie films.

Mercado de San Ildefonso:

Where? Malasaña, Madrid's hipster heartland.
What? Three floors of pure gastronomic pleasure, from tapas bars to cocktail spots.

How to Get There: Metro: Tribunal station.

Local's Tip: Perfect for a late evening. The vibe starts getting electric post 8 pm!

Mercado de Motores:
Where? Paseo de la Delicias.
What? A monthly market held inside a railway museum. Vintage finds, handcrafted jewelry, and so much more.

How to Get There: Metro: Delicias station.

Local's Tip: Reach early! This market is monthly, so it gets pretty packed.

Madrileño 101: Navigating the Nuances of Madrid Life

To truly vibe with Madrid, you need more than just a fancy phrasebook or a craving for paella. Let's dive into the less-talked-about, day-to-day etiquettes of this vibrant city, so you don't just visit Madrid – you live Madrid!

1. **The Madrid Hello:**
   Nope, a simple 'hi' won't cut it here. When in Madrid, do as the Madrileños do: two kisses, one on each cheek (right to left). It's

common between men and women or between women. Men generally stick to hearty handshakes amongst themselves.

Local's Tip: This is mostly among friends. With strangers, a smile and a 'hola' is golden.

2. **Taking Your Time:**
   Rushing your meal? That's sacrilege! Enjoying food is almost a ceremony here. Meals are times to relax, chat, and take in the ambiance. So, breathe deep and savor each bite.

   Local's Tip: Lunch, especially, is a lengthy affair. Don't be surprised if it's a 2-3 hour event!

3. **Being Vocal is Normal:**
   Madrileños are a passionate bunch! They might seem loud during conversations, but that's just them being expressive. Don't mistake it for aggression.

   Local's Tip: Feel free to jump in the conversation. Just remember, it's all in good spirit!

4. **Dress the Part:**
   While Madrid is cosmopolitan, locals tend to dress more formally, especially in the evenings. Ditch those flip-flops for a good pair of shoes.

   Local's Tip: It's always better to be slightly overdressed than under. Plus, Madrileños take pride in their appearance!

5. **Tipping isn't a Top Priority:**
   Unlike some cultures where tipping is obligatory, in Madrid, it's more of a gesture. If you liked the service, leave some change, but there's no fixed percentage.

Local's Tip: At a cafe, rounding up or leaving a few coins is appreciated. At a nicer restaurant, maybe a euro or two.

Things to Remember:

Queueing: Madrileños aren't the biggest fans of orderly lines, especially in busier places. Hold your ground (politely)!
Nightlife: The party starts late and ends with the sunrise. So, rest up for the long haul!
Language Courtesy: While many people speak English, starting any conversation with "¿Hablas inglés?" (Do you speak English?) is always a polite touch.

Key Takeaways

- Highlighted dishes: Cocido Madrileño, Bocadillo de Calamares, Oreja a la Plancha, Churros con Chocolate, Rosquillas de San Isidro, Sopa de Ajo, Huevos Rotos, and Torrijas.
- Madrileños dine late due to historical, cultural, and geographical reasons.
- Highlighted nightlife venues: Casa Patas, Círculo de Bellas Artes Rooftop Bar, Mondo Disko, Mercado de San Ildefonso, and El Estudio.
- Madrid has various lesser-known festivals that provide an authentic experience.
- Featured festivals: Fiesta de la Trashumancia, Fiesta de San Cayetano, Noche de los Teatros, and Fiesta de la Almudena.
- Madrid's local markets offer unique shopping experiences beyond the typical tourist spots.
- Highlighted markets: Mercado de la Paz, Mercado de San Fernando, and Antón Martín Market.

Action Steps

✓ **Digital Map:** Create a custom Google Map marking each recommended eatery.
- o Pin spots for Cocido Madrileño, Bocadillo de Calamares, and so on.
- o Color-code for easy differentiation: e.g., blue for vegan spots.

✓ **Meal Planner:** Use an app like Trello to organize meals:
- o Assign a dish or eatery for each day of the trip.
- o Attach a photo of the dish to whet your appetite!

✓ **Local Ingredient Hunt:** Visit local markets to source ingredients for a DIY Spanish meal.
- o Chat with locals for best ingredient tips.

✓ **Interactive Festival Checklist:** Use apps like Todoist to:
- o List all festivals happening during your visit.
- o Set reminders a day ahead.

✓ **Social Media Alerts:** Set Google or Twitter alerts for festival hashtags.
- o Get real-time festival updates or flash events.

✓ **Local Interaction:** Try the app "Tandem" to:
- o Connect with locals willing to share festival insights.
- o Maybe even find a festival buddy!

✓ **Augmented Reality (AR) Assistance:** Use AR apps to:
- o Virtually try on clothes or accessories in markets.
- o Get instant reviews or product details.

✓ **Digital Payment:** Ensure you have mobile payment methods set up:
- o Apple Pay, Google Wallet, or similar for quick transactions.

✓ **Eco-conscious Shopping:** Download an eco-rating app to:
- o Check product sustainability scores while shopping.
- o Make environmentally friendly choices.

✓ **Transportation Pro:** Use Citymapper or Moovit to:
  - o Plan efficient routes using public transport.
  - o Get live updates on metro timings.
✓ **Digital Journaling:** Use apps like Day One or Journey to:
  - o Document daily experiences, photos, and reflections.
  - o Create a digital memento of the Madrid trip.

Conclusion

Hey there, traveler! You've made it through our tour of Madrid, and what a ride it's been, right?

Let's take a quick look back and remember some cool things we've discovered about this incredible city.

Recap Time:

History in Every Corner: Remember when we talked about Madrid's history? It's not just about old buildings and dusty tales. Every corner, from the Royal Palace to La Latina, whispers stories. Think about those cobblestone streets; people have been walking them for centuries, each leaving their mark.

Food Adventures: From our delicious deep dive into Madrid's foods – Cocido Madrileño, Churros, Tapas, oh my! – we realized that food isn't just fuel. It's an emotion. It's a memory. It's that sweet moment of your day.

Artsy Vibes: Art isn't just framed in Madrid. It's on the streets, in the air, in the sounds. The Prado Museum and the graffiti on the alley walls show the same thing: Madrid has creativity in its veins.

Party Time: Night owls, this one's for you. Madrid knows how to throw a party. From traditional flamenco to those edgy nightclubs, there's always a beat to dance to.

Madrid Tomorrow: This city isn't stuck in the past. It's dreaming about the future, trying out new stuff, being all innovative, and still keeping its cool, old-world charm.

But here's the thing. Reading a guide is like checking out the menu at a restaurant. You get a feel, but you haven't really tasted anything yet. Madrid isn't just about stories on paper; it's about the ones you'll create.

What Now?:

Alright, buddy. It's action time. Don't just daydream about Madrid. Dive in! Chat with the locals, taste that churro, dance like no one's watching, and maybe even pick up a word or two in Spanish. Make those stories. And hey, don't forget to grab your sneakers. There's a lot of ground to cover.

Madrid has given you a peek into its heart. It's your turn now. Make memories, laugh out loud, get lost (sometimes on purpose), and soak in every moment. And when you feel like it's time for a new story, Barcelona's just around the corner, waiting with its own set of tales.

One More Thing...:

Travel isn't just about hopping from one spot to another. It's about growth. The Madrid chapter has hopefully added a few more layers to your story, given you fresh perspectives, and maybe even changed the way you look at the world. And just remember, as you turn this page, a brand-new chapter awaits in Barcelona. It's calling, with its bustling streets, shimmering beaches, and tales of its own.

Adventure is a lifelong journey. Madrid was a stop, a beautiful one, but there are more horizons to chase. So, strap on those boots, grab that map, and keep that spirit alive.

Stay curious, traveler. The world's a book, and you've got many more pages to turn. Safe journeys, and here's to the next grand adventure!

BOOK 2

Barcelona Travel Guide

Explore to Win

Introduction

"There is no passion to be found playing small - in settling for a life that is less than the one you are capable of living."
- Nelson Mandela

Do you remember the thrill of your first solo ride on a bicycle? The wind against your face, the sheer joy of movement? That's Barcelona but magnified by a thousand. It's a city that promises you more than just sights. It promises experiences. It promises growth. But wait, if Barcelona is this bike ride, where's the roadmap? Ah, that's where we come in!

You've felt it, haven't you? That distressing feeling of not wanting just another vacation, but a meaningful journey. The pain point of flipping through countless blogs, guides, and Instagram posts, only to be overwhelmed by the sheer volume of 'must-dos'. How do you separate the authentic from the touristy? How do you ensure your experience in Barcelona isn't just a checklist, but a tale worth telling?

This book is more than a guide; it's your compass. With it, you'll:

- **Discover Hidden Gems:** Those alleys, terraces, and local haunts that aren't teeming with tourists. The real, undiluted Barcelona.

- **Connect with the Locals:** Dive deep into the Catalonian culture. Understand their festivals, their traditions, and the stories that shaped them.

- **Save Time and Money:** Get tips that keep you away from tourist traps and scams. Enjoy the best of Barcelona without burning a hole in your pocket.

- **Personal Growth:** Barcelona's not just a place; it's a lesson. Learn the art of slow travel, of truly immersing oneself, and returning richer in experience and perspective.

Now, you might wonder, "Why trust this guide? What makes it different?"

Simply put, this guide isn't just researched; it's lived. While I might not have a PhD in Catalonian history, my love affair with Barcelona spans over a decade. It started with a three-day trip and transformed into yearly pilgrimages, each more enlightening than the last. From my first taste of 'pa amb tomàquet' at a bustling local market to dancing in the city's grand La Mercè festival, I've savored Barcelona in its raw, unfiltered form. Each chapter is a labor of love, a mosaic of personal experiences, local interactions, and rigorous research.

But more than anything, this guide serves you, the reader. It's tailored for those who seek depth in their travels. If you're looking for a cursory glance at the city's top 5 attractions, this might not be for you. But if you're keen on understanding Barcelona, feeling its pulse, and returning with stories that not everyone tells, then you're in the right place.

Before you dive in, a word of advice: travel, at its best, is unplanned. While this guide provides you the tools, the adventure is yours to craft. Let curiosity be your guide, and serendipity, your companion.

Feeling the flutter of excitement? Good! Hold on to that feeling. As you turn the page, the Catalonian capital awaits with its tapestry of tales, flavors, and moments.

In the next chapter, we begin our journey not with the most popular, but with the most authentic. We'll delve into Barcelona's heart. From the historic charm of El Raval to the beachy vibes of Barceloneta, get ready to step into the stories that make Barcelona, well, Barcelona.

Ready to make your Barcelona journey legendary? Vamos!

Chapter 1: Hidden Gems of Barcelona

"To awaken quite alone in a strange town is one of the pleasantest sensations in the world."
- Freya Stark

Hey there, fellow wanderer!

So, you've decided to plunge into the world of Barcelona. A city famed for its architectural marvels, sun-drenched beaches, and football frenzy, right? But let me tell you, as someone who's been there, done that, and got the T-shirt (literally!), Barcelona has so much more to offer beneath its shiny surface.

You know, everyone talks about La Sagrada Familia, Las Ramblas, and the streets of the Gothic Quarter. And sure, they're beautiful, iconic, and totally Instagram-worthy. But Barcelona's true magic? It's in the places that aren't swarming with tourists, where the true essence of Catalan culture unfurls like a hidden tapestry, waiting to be discovered.

In this chapter, we're diving deep. Not into the usual, but into the streets less wandered. The quaint cafes tucked in forgotten alleys, the art nooks that only locals know about, and those silent spots where you can hear the heartbeat of this vibrant city. Think of this chapter as your secret map, your treasure hunt guide to Barcelona's hidden wonders.

El Poblenou's Industrial Charm

Imagine a place where the vestiges of a bustling industrial past meet the vibrancy of contemporary art, culture, and technology. Sounds intriguing, right? Welcome to El Poblenou, Barcelona's best-kept secret and my favorite spot to lose myself in.

Why El Poblenou? Once the industrial heart of Barcelona, today, this neighborhood brims with artists' studios, tech startups, and some seriously cool urban beaches. Its transformation is a testament to how innovation and art can breathe new life into the old.

Local Tips:

- **Mingle with the locals**: Skip the Starbucks and head to one of the local cafes. Try a cortado (an espresso cut with a small amount of warm milk). You'll not only get a feel for the local scene but also some seriously good coffee.

- **Visit on the Second Weekend:** Why? Because of the "Poblenou Open Day," when artists open their studios to the public. It's a rare treat to watch these creators in their element.

What to Do:

- **Rambla del Poblenou:** It's the neighborhood's main street and a less crowded alternative to La Rambla. Wander through, soak in the atmosphere, and don't forget to grab some churros.

- **Poblenou Urban District:** A hub of contemporary art. From street art to art galleries like La Plataforma, there's a lot to absorb.

- **Torre Agbar:** While not exactly in El Poblenou, this modern skyscraper is on its border and offers a stunning panoramic view of the city.

Where to Go:

- **Can Framis Museum:** A former textile factory, now a contemporary art museum. The blend of old architecture with modern art is a visual treat.

- **Palo Market Fest:** Held on the first weekend of every month, this is where you can find handcrafted local products, live music, and some delicious street food.

- **When to Go:** Spring and fall are the best times. Not too hot, not too crowded, and the district's creative events are in full swing.

How to Get There:

- **Metro:** Take the L4 line and get off at Poblenou station.
- **Bike:** If you're staying in central Barcelona, rent a bike. The ride to Poblenou along the beach is absolutely scenic.

Laberint d'Horta: Barcelona's Oldest Preserved Garden

Close your eyes and imagine a place in Barcelona where time seems to stand still, where myth and reality blend seamlessly. Can you picture walking through a labyrinth, surrounded by tall, verdant hedges with the thrill of discovery at every twist and turn? Welcome to Laberint d'Horta, a tranquil slice of heaven right in the middle of bustling Barcelona.

Why Laberint d'Horta? Built in the 18th century, this historic garden showcases neoclassical and romantic designs. Beyond its alluring maze, it offers peaceful spots, water features, and sculptures that transport you straight into a fairytale.

Local Tips:

- **Early Bird Gets the Worm:** The garden is most serene in the early morning. Plus, you beat the tourist rush!

- **Snap That Pic:** The center of the maze boasts a romantic statue. Find your way there, and don't forget to snap a commemorative photo.

What to Do:

- **The Labyrinth:** It's the star of the show! Navigate its twists and turns, and feel the rush of making it to the center.

- **Sculpture Hunt:** The gardens are dotted with statues from Greek mythology. Challenge yourself to identify them all!

- **Pond Relaxation:** There are tranquil ponds where ducks happily waddle. Perfect for a few moments of relaxation.

Where to Go:

- **The Romantic Garden:** A space with tall trees, waterfalls, and flowerbeds. The perfect place to read a book or daydream.

- **The Pavilion:** Overlooking the maze, it's the best spot to get a bird's eye view and maybe help out lost wanderers below.

- **When to Go:** Spring is magical, with flowers in full bloom. However, fall offers a golden hue, with fewer visitors and a mellow ambiance.

How to Get There:

- **Metro:** Hop onto the L3 line and disembark at Mundet station. A short walk, and you're there!
- **Bus:** Several buses, like 27, 60, and 73, can drop you close to the garden's entrance.

Hospital de Sant Pau: An Architectural Wonder Off the Beaten Path

Have you ever stumbled upon a hidden gem that made you wonder how such a marvel could stay so quietly tucked away? If La Sagrada Familia is the roaring lion of Barcelona's architectural landscape, think of Hospital de Sant Pau as its regal, yet understated, counterpart.

Why Hospital de Sant Pau? Initially functioning as a hospital until the late 20th century, this structure redefines the intersection of art and utility. Designed by Lluís Domènech i Montaner, it stands as a testament to Modernisme architecture – it's as if Gaudí had a lesser-known sibling, equally talented and vividly imaginative.

Local Tips:

- **Eyes to the Sky:** The intricate facades and colorful mosaics are a photographer's dream. Look up and capture those details!

- **Guided Tours:** The inside is just as fascinating. Opt for a guided tour to truly appreciate its architectural and historical significance.

What to Do:

- **Architecture Appreciation:** Revel in the blend of Gothic and Art Nouveau styles, with angels, dragons, and nature-inspired motifs at every corner.

- **Gardens & Courtyards:** Amidst the 12 pavilions, each has its unique courtyard. Perfect spots to relax and ponder the genius of Montaner.

- **Exhibitions:** Often, parts of the hospital host exhibitions and cultural events. Check ahead and enrich your experience.

Where to Go:

- **Sant Rafael Pavilion:** A central building with a plethora of stories and a rich history.

- **Underground Tunnels:** Once connecting various parts of the hospital, now they offer a unique exploration experience.

When to Go:

- While mornings can be quieter, the soft glow of the evening sun accentuates the hospital's beauty.

How to Get There:

- **Metro:** The L5 line will be your best friend. Alight at the Sant Pau | Dos de Maig station.

- **Bus:** Buses like 19, 47, and 117 conveniently stop close by.

Bunkers del Carmel: Panoramic Views Beyond Your Wildest Dreams

You're on top of the world! Or at least, it feels that way. The entirety of Barcelona stretches out before you, a mosaic of rooftops, spires, and the glistening Mediterranean in the distance. This isn't a dream—it's the reality at Bunkers del Carmel, one of Barcelona's best-kept secrets.

Why Bunkers del Carmel? Originally built during the Spanish Civil War for defense purposes, this spot has now transformed into a favorite vantage point for locals and a handful of savvy travelers. Minimalistic in its current infrastructure, its real charm lies in the unparalleled 360-degree views of the city.

Local Tips:

- **Sunrise or Sunset:** Want a backdrop that's straight out of a postcard? Time your visit for golden hour.

- **Picnic:** This is the spot! Grab some local cheese, olives, and a bottle of cava for an impromptu picnic.

What to Do:

- **Photo Session:** Every angle offers a unique view of Barcelona. Capture memories with the Sagrada Familia, Montjuic, and the beach all in one frame.

- **Historic Musings:** Reflect on the area's history. From bunkers to the best city viewpoint, it's a transformation to appreciate.

- **Local Interaction:** Often, you'll find local musicians strumming away. Take a moment to enjoy the melodies and maybe even join in a dance!

Where to Go:

- **Turó de la Rovira:** The hill on which the bunkers are situated. A trek, but worth every step.

- **Nearby Parks:** After descending, relax in one of the parks nestled in the El Carmel neighborhood.

- **When to Go:** Weekdays are usually less crowded. For a serene experience, early mornings are key!

How to Get There:

- **Bus:** V17 will take you pretty close. From there, it's a steep walk, so wear comfy shoes!
- **Walking:** If you're up for it, the journey from Park Güell is scenic and rewarding.

Mercat de la Boqueria: A Culinary Odyssey Off La Rambla

Imagine strolling through a bustling market, colors popping from every stall, the aroma of fresh produce, meats, and spices playfully teasing your senses. Your taste buds do a little dance in anticipation. Welcome to Mercat de la Boqueria, a culinary wonderland hidden just off the famous La Rambla.

Why Mercat de la Boqueria? Going beyond the regular tourist trails, this market is where tradition meets modern gastronomy. It's not just a market; it's an experience.

Local Tips:

Stall Selection: Seek out stalls run by families who've been here for generations. Their knowledge of their produce and passion is unmatched.

Tasting Counters: Many stalls have tiny counters where you can sample dishes. Don't be shy; dive right in.

What to Do:

Tapas Trail: Navigate through a maze of stalls and pick different tapas. Create your tapas trail and indulge!

Fresh Juices: Scattered throughout the market are stalls selling fresh fruit juices in a kaleidoscope of colors. From tropical coconut-pineapple to the vibrant dragon fruit, it's a refreshing pit-stop.

Chocolatiers: For those with a sweet tooth, some stalls specialize in handmade chocolates. Bite into Barcelona's sweet side!

Where to Go:

Fish Lane: An entire lane dedicated to seafood. Watch as fishmongers display the day's freshest catch.

Organic Corner: Looking for organic and specialty items? Head over to this section, where eco-friendly meets delicious.

When to Go: Early mornings are the most active, with locals doing their daily shopping. It's a vibrant experience minus the massive tourist crowds.

How to Get There:

Walking: The market entrance is right off La Rambla, making it easily accessible on foot from various parts of the city.

Metro: Liceu station on the L3 line drops you just a stone's throw away from the market.

Casa Vicens: Gaudí's Forgotten Masterpiece

Let me paint a scene for you. A house unlike any other stands in a quiet corner of Gràcia. A mosaic of colors, patterns, and art forms from various cultures come together. This isn't just any house; it's Gaudí's first significant work in Barcelona. Meet Casa Vicens, the overshadowed sibling of the more famous Gaudí creations.

Why Casa Vicens? While everyone flocks to La Sagrada Familia and Parc Güell, Casa Vicens offers an intimate look into the mind of the genius at the beginning of his career.

Local Tips:

- **Photography:** The facade, adorned with vibrant tiles and intricate ironwork, is a dream for photographers. The garden is a little oasis too!

- **Guided Tours:** Consider opting for one. The stories and insights offered can enhance the whole experience.

What to Do:

- **Explore the Rooms:** Each room is a marvel, showcasing Gaudí's experimentation with styles and materials.

- **Rooftop Views:** Climb up for a panoramic view of the city, with the added bonus of seeing Gaudí's chimneys up close.

- **Relax in the Garden:** A space designed to be an extension of the home, with beautiful tiles and plants. A quiet moment here is like stepping back in time.

- **When to Go:** Late afternoons are ideal. The setting sun casts a golden hue, perfect for capturing those Instagram-worthy shots.

How to Get There:

- **Walking:** Gràcia is a delightful neighborhood to walk through, with its bohemian vibes and narrow streets leading to Casa Vicens.

- **Metro:** The L3 line to Fontana or the L4 to Joanic are the closest metro stops. A short walk from either station will take you to the gem.

Key Takeaways

- **El Poblenou's:** A unique blend of industrial heritage and modern art, Poblenou is a testament to Barcelona's evolution and a must-visit for culture enthusiasts.

- **Laberint d'Horta:** A journey through Barcelona's oldest garden maze is a serene escape from the city bustle, offering history and nature in one spot.

- **Hospital de Sant Pau:** Beyond its function as a medical facility, this site showcases architectural brilliance that rivals the more famous landmarks, revealing a quieter side of Gaudí-inspired designs.

- **Mercat de la Boqueria:** A sensory delight, this market goes beyond fresh produce to offer a glimpse into the daily life and rich gastronomy of Barcelona.

- **Bunkers del Carmel:** Elevated views and a taste of history converge at this spot, presenting an unmatched panoramic vista of the city beneath.

- **Casa Vicens:** Gaudí's first major architectural marvel, this house introduces visitors to the beginnings of his distinct style, setting the stage for his later, more recognized works.

Action Steps & Tips

✓ Research Ahead: Before you head out, double-check opening hours and any entrance fees. Some spots might have specific visitor guidelines or special events.

✓ Go Early: Beat the crowds and get to these gems during the early hours. Not only will you enjoy a more serene experience, but the lighting for photographs will be optimal.

✓ Local Guidance: Always ask locals for their personal tips about visiting these spots. They might know the best times, vantage points, or even little-known facts.

✓ Comfort First: Wear comfortable walking shoes. Many of these gems involve a good deal of walking or are located on uneven terrains.

✓ Stay Hydrated and Snacked: Carry a reusable water bottle and some local snacks. Especially when exploring places like Laberint d'Horta or Bunkers del Carmel, you'll appreciate having refreshments on hand.

✓ Respect the Space: Remember, many of these locations are cherished by locals. Always be respectful by not littering and keeping noise levels down.

✓ Capture Memories: Don't forget your camera! But also, take moments to simply absorb the beauty without any lens in between.

✓ Stay Connected: Consider getting a local SIM card or portable Wi-Fi. It'll help you navigate, translate, or look up information on-the-go.

✓ Stay Updated: Some spots might occasionally close for private events or maintenance. It's always a good idea to check their official website or local news sources before heading out.

✓ Enjoy the Journey: While the destinations are magnificent, don't forget to enjoy the journey. The streets of Barcelona are filled with charm at every corner.

Chapter 2: Day Trips Worth the Detour

"Life begins at the end of your comfort zone."
- Neale Donald Walsch

Okay, adventure-seeker, so you've wined, dined, and salsa-ed your way through the narrow alleys of Barcelona and ticked off a bunch of those hidden gems from our last chapter. Feeling pretty chuffed, are we? Well, hold onto your tapas because we're about to shake things up a bit!

Ever thought about discovering a place where the mountains kiss the sky? Or maybe a hidden beach where the waves playfully tease the shores? How about a vineyard where each grape holds a story? Get ready to have your socks knocked off (or sandals, considering the weather) because this chapter is all about taking that little detour to find big adventures. So, grab your day pack, a good pair of sneakers, and perhaps a cheeky snack or two (I'm all about those churros, baby!), and let's hit the road!

Montserrat

Let's set the scene. Jagged mountains that seem to pierce the sky, an ancient monastery perched precariously on a cliff, and views that'll make you whip out your phone faster than you can say "Instagram-worthy". Welcome to Montserrat!

The Local Lowdown:

- **The Name:** No, Montserrat isn't named after a tropical bird. The name translates to "Serrated Mountain" in Catalan, thanks to the unique jagged rock formations.
- **The Legends:** Listen closely, and you might just hear locals whispering tales of the Black Madonna, an iconic statue housed in the monastery and a beacon for pilgrims worldwide.

How to Get There:

- **By Train:** Board the R5 train from Barcelona's Plaça Espanya to Aeri de Montserrat. From there, opt for the cable car to reach the mountain's summit. Enjoy those views!
- **By Car:** If you're road-tripping, it's roughly an hour's drive. Plug "Montserrat Monastery" into your GPS, and off you go!

Top Tips:

- **Beat the Crowds:** Aim to arrive early, preferably by 10 a.m., to dodge those big tourist groups and have the pathways to yourself.
- **Dress Wisely:** While the monastery isn't super strict, it's best to wear respectful attire (think covered shoulders). Also, pack layers – the mountain's elevation means it can get chilly.
- **Snack Attack:** Bring some snacks and water. The on-site eateries can be a tad pricey.

Activities Not to Miss (seriously, don't!):

- **The Monastery:** Beyond its spiritual significance, its architecture is a visual treat.

- **Hiking Trails:** If you're itching for some physical activity, Montserrat has trails galore. The path to Sant Jeroni offers particularly gasp-inducing views.
- **Listen to the Boys' Choir:** 'Escolania de Montserrat' is one of Europe's oldest boys' choirs. Their angelic voices in the basilica? Total goosebumps moment.

Local Must-Tries:

- **Mató Cheese:** A soft cheese typically drizzled with honey. It's a Montserrat special and, trust me, it's delish.
- **Liqueurs:** Monks have been brewing herbal liqueurs here for ages. Why not grab a bottle as a souvenir?

Parting Wisdom:

- Set aside a full day. Between the monastery, hikes, and just soaking in the views, you'll need it.
- Always check the local calendar. Montserrat often hosts events and festivals which can either add to the charm or the crowds.

Sitges

Picture me shimmying in excitement as I tell you about this next spot! Imagine a quaint coastal town where golden sands meet crystal clear waters while narrow cobblestone streets tell tales of history and culture. Drumroll, please... Welcome to Sitges!

The Local Lowdown:

- **The Vibe:** Think of Sitges as Barcelona's laid-back cousin who loves art, parties during Carnaval like there's no tomorrow, and takes afternoon siestas by the sea.

- **History Check:** Sitges was once a refuge for artists and writers; its bohemian spirit still lingers today, and it proudly waves the rainbow flag as an LGBTQ+ friendly destination.

Getting There:

- **By Train:** From Barcelona, grab the RENFE train R2 south from Estació de Sants. Within 40 minutes, you'll be breathing in that sweet sea air.
- **By Car:** About a 45-minute drive. Remember to look out for "parquímetros" – parking meters, so you don't get a sneaky ticket!

Top Tips:

- **When to Go:** If you're a party enthusiast, February's Carnaval is unforgettable. For a more serene vibe, consider September when the town's Film Festival rolls out the red carpet.
- **Beach Bum Tip:** Balmins Beach is a lovely spot and... it's nudist! So, either bare it all or just enjoy the freedom around.
- **Pack a Hat:** Sitges is sunny, like, A LOT. So, sunscreen and a hat are non-negotiable.

Activities That'll Make Your Heart Sing:

- **Cau Ferrat Museum:** Once home to the artist Santiago Rusiñol, it's now a museum showcasing modernist art.
- **Promenade Strolls:** The Passeig Maritim is a long seaside promenade. Perfect for sunset walks!
- **Attend a 'Correfoc':** This traditional fire-running event is thrilling! But, dress appropriately – think protective clothing to dance among the sparks!

Local Delights to Satisfy Those Taste Buds:

- **Xató Salad:** A local salad with a special sauce made of almonds, hazelnuts, and ñora peppers. An explosion of flavor!
- **Malvasia Wine:** A sweet dessert wine that has been produced in the region for centuries. It's like a hug in a glass.

And Before You Scoot Off:

- Rent a bike. It's one of the best ways to explore Sitges and its lovely surroundings.
- Engage with locals. They're friendly and always have the juiciest recommendations that no guidebook will tell you.

Girona

Have you ever wished to step into a time machine and be whisked away to a medieval realm? Well, grab your imaginary cloak and goblet because Girona is your next enchanting stop!

The Local Lowdown:

- **The Vibe:** Girona feels like a dreamy blend of the past and present, where ancient walls guard modern day secrets.
- **Didja Know?:** Ever heard of a tiny show called 'Game of Thrones'? Well, parts of it were filmed right here, in Girona's winding alleys and grand plazas!

Getting There (Hang tight, no dragons involved):

- **By Train:** A quick journey from Barcelona, Girona is just about 40 minutes away via the high-speed AVE train.
- **By Car:** A smooth 1.5-hour drive from Barcelona. Medieval charm, here you come!

Top Tips:

- **When to Go:** Visit during the 'Temps de Flors' in May. The city turns into a vibrant floral fiesta!
- **Girona Cards:** They offer free public transport and discounts to major attractions. A traveler's jackpot.
- **Elevated Views:** Climb the city walls for a panoramic view. You might just spot a dragon or two (wink).

Must-Dos:

- **Cathedral of Saint Mary:** Not only an iconic 'GoT' spot but also home to the widest Gothic nave in the world!
- **Jewish Quarter:** Dive into narrow lanes that echo with tales from centuries past.
- **Onyar River Houses:** Capture the Instagram-worthy colorful houses that reflect beautifully in the river.

For Your Gastronomic Pleasure:

- **Coca de llardons:** A delicious local pastry you'd regret not tasting.
- **Ratafia:** Cheers with this traditional liqueur that carries the spirit of Girona in every sip.

Before You Bid Adieu:

- Pop by the Girona Film Museum for an unexpected cinematic treat.
- The Eiffel Bridge: Yes, related to THAT Eiffel. A picture-perfect spot to wrap up your visit.

El Raval

Fancy a detour from the touristy tracks? El Raval has got you covered with its unique blend of bohemian spirit, historic haunts, and a cosmopolitan crowd. Come along; there's a world to uncover here!

Unraveling El Raval:

- **Local Vibe:** Think of an old record store meeting a contemporary art studio. Raw, eclectic, and buzzing - that's El Raval in a nutshell.
- **Did You Know?:** El Raval once had a naughty reputation, but oh boy, how it has transformed! Today, it's a melting pot of cultures and arts.

Getting to El Raval:

- **By Metro:** Drassanes, Liceu, and Paral·lel metro stations are your gateways to this vibrant neighborhood.
- **On Foot:** Nestled right next to La Rambla, a leisurely walk will lead you to the heart of El Raval.

Local Tips to Boost Your Raval Rendezvous:

- **Best Time to Visit:** Early evening. Watch El Raval come alive as the sun sets, with music, chatter, and clinks of glasses.
- **Safety First:** While much safer now, always be cautious of your belongings.
- **Street Art Alert:** This place is a graffiti paradise. So, camera-ready?

Must-See Spots in El Raval:

- **MACBA (Museum of Contemporary Art of Barcelona):** Modern art in an ultra-modern building.
- **Rambla del Raval:** A broad boulevard teeming with terraces, tapas bars, and a super selfie-friendly giant cat sculpture by Botero.
- **Hospital de la Santa Creu:** An old hospital with cloisters that ooze tranquility.

For the Foodies:

- **Bar Marsella:** Step into this iconic bar, rumored to have once served absinthe to Picasso and Hemingway.
- **Elisabets:** Craving traditional Catalan dishes? Your taste buds will thank you here.

Before Waving Goodbye:

- Pop into any of the vintage stores; there's always a quirky find awaiting.
- Sala Apolo: If you're in the mood for some dancing, this iconic spot hosts fantastic gigs and club nights.

Poble Sec

Welcome, explorer, to the lively neighborhood of Poble Sec! Here's where tradition dances with the trend, and every street corner has a story to tell. It's time to don your walking shoes, join the locals, and get ready to feast on all things Poble Sec.

What's Poble Sec all about?

- **Local Vibe:** A joyful juxtaposition of trendy eateries, old-school tapas bars, and vibrant street life, Poble Sec offers a flavor of Barcelona that's both grounded and glam.
- **Historical Peek:** Once a working-class neighborhood, today's Poble Sec retains its gritty charm while embracing a fresh burst of creativity.

Navigating Poble Sec:

By Metro: Poble Sec Metro station is your go-to spot. Jump on Line 3, and you're there.
On Foot: If you're around Montjuïc, a leisurely walk downhill leads you straight into Poble Sec.

A Handful of Handy Local Tips:

Best Time to Visit: Come evening, as the sun dips, and the streets come alive with locals, laughter, and lots of tapas.
Tapas Trail: Don't miss the legendary Carrer de Blai for its endless row of tapas bars. Pinchos, anyone?
Nightlife Niche: From jazz clubs to trendy bars, Poble Sec doesn't sleep early.

Poble Sec's Signature Spots:

Teatre Grec: An open-air amphitheater offering delightful performances, set against the backdrop of lush gardens.
Sala Apolo: If your feet itch to dance, you know where to go!
Mercat de Sant Antoni: A market teeming with life, fresh produce, and hidden culinary treasures.

Culinary Corner:

Quimet & Quimet: A tiny spot with towering flavors. Try their unique montaditos, little bites that pack a punch.
Bar Ramón: Old-school decor, new-age vibe. Don't leave without tasting their legendary bravas.

Winding Down:

Wander through the Parallel Avenue, a historical theater street, catching a glimpse of the city's performing arts heritage.
Relax at the Montjuïc's Magic Fountain; the nightly shows are a visual treat.
And that, dear friend, is Poble Sec in a vibrant nutshell! An urban tapestry woven with art, food, culture, and that irresistible Catalonian charm. What's next, you ask? Oh, there's more to explore. Shall we?

Key Takeaways

- Montserrat: A spiritual sanctuary atop majestic mountains; visit early in the day to beat the crowds, and don't miss the funicular ride for breathtaking views.

- Sitges: A coastal charm just a train ride away; the best time is during the carnival or the film festival, but any summer day promises sun-kissed fun.

- Girona: Step back in time in this historic city; visit during the Temps de Flors festival for a floral feast or just wander the medieval walls for a quiet, reflective day.

- Poble Sec: Where tradition meets trend; explore this lively neighborhood in the evening, follow the tapas trail, and embrace the bustling nightlife.

- El Raval: A melting pot of cultures and creativity; art enthusiasts should target the contemporary museums, while foodies can savor the diverse culinary scene.

These destinations offer a blend of unique experiences and cultures, all within a day's reach from Barcelona. Your adventure can be as laid-back or as lively as you choose, but these insights will ensure you're in sync with the local vibe and can make the most of your trips. Happy exploring!

Action Steps

- Research train or bus schedules to ensure a smooth journey to Montserrat, Sitges, and Girona. Local transportation can have varying schedules, especially on weekends.
- Bring appropriate clothing and accessories for the day's activities. A hat and sunscreen for Sitges' beaches, comfortable walking shoes for Girona's cobbled streets, or a light jacket for Montserrat's cooler mountain air.
- Engage with local traditions. Try "xató" in Sitges, or join a guided tour of Girona's Jewish Quarter. Visit local bars in Poble Sec for authentic tapas.
- Consider visiting Montserrat on weekdays to avoid crowds, and check local festival dates in Sitges and Girona to coincide with your trip.
- Wander around El Raval's hidden art galleries, or hike lesser-known trails in Montserrat for unique vistas.
- For popular attractions or guided tours, especially during peak seasons, it might be wise to book in advance.

Chapter 3: Modern Traveler in Barcelona

"Traveling is seeing; it is the implicit that we travel by."
-Cynthia Ozick

The modern traveler - gallant, gadget-loaded, and occasionally GPS-lost. If you've ever wondered how to blend into Barcelona like a local without whipping out a massive paper map or asking for Wi-Fi passwords in broken Spanish, you're in the right place.

The streets of Barcelona are filled with centuries-old history, but that doesn't mean you have to travel like it's 1492. From digital wallets to ride-sharing apps, and from trendy co-working spaces to eco-friendly travel options, the city is filled with modern conveniences that make exploring this Catalonian gem a breeze.

Get ready to navigate Barcelona in style, with all the digital savvy of a 21st-century explorer. And don't worry, we'll keep the technical jargon to a minimum – we want you to enjoy your trip, not prepare for an IT exam!

Mobile Payment Options

Apple Pay

If you're an iPhone enthusiast, then you'll be pleased to know that Apple Pay is widely accepted across the city. Here's how to navigate it like a local:

Setup: Before you hit the streets, make sure Apple Pay is set up on your device and linked to your bank. Some Spanish banks might require additional verification, so be sure to check that before you leave your country.

Usage: From small cafés to large shopping centers, Apple Pay is your contactless friend. Just look for the contactless symbol at the checkout.

Local Tip: Many local markets, especially those off the beaten path, may still prefer cash, so keep some euros handy just in case.

Venmo

While Venmo is primarily a U.S. service, you may still find ways to utilize it in Barcelona, particularly among other travelers or expats. Here's what you need to know:

Sending Money: It's an easy way to split bills with friends or fellow travelers. Enjoyed a group tapas feast? Venmo makes paying your share a breeze.

Receiving Payments: Sold an old guitar to a fellow expat in the Gothic Quarter? Venmo's got you covered.

Local Insight: Venmo isn't as widely used among the locals, so don't rely on it for everyday purchases. Instead, think of it as a handy tool for those unique situations.

Convenience and Safety

Mobile payments in Barcelona not only bring convenience but also an added layer of safety. No more fumbling with cash or cards, just tap and go. Remember, though:

Security: Always use secure Wi-Fi connections when handling financial transactions.

Back-Up Plan: Have a physical card handy, as not all places accept mobile payments. That little churros shop tucked away in El Born might still be cash-only!

Charges and Fees: Check with your bank about any international transaction fees associated with mobile payments to avoid surprises.

Transportation Apps

Uber in Barcelona

Getting around Barcelona is now easier than ever with Uber. Here's how you can ride like a local:

Booking: Open the app, enter your destination, and voila! Your ride is on the way.

Local Tip: Uber isn't as widespread as in some other cities, but you'll still find it handy for airport trips or late-night rides.

Alternative: If Uber isn't your thing, apps like Cabify offer similar services.

Metro App (TMB App)

Barcelona's Metro is efficient and extensive. The TMB app makes it even easier:

Routes and Times: Plan your journey and check train times.

Tickets: Buy your tickets directly from the app.

Local Insight: During peak times, trains can be crowded. Plan accordingly!

Moovit

Navigate the Network: Moovit provides real-time updates on buses, trains, and trams. It offers step-by-step navigation, making it easy to travel like a local.
Service Alerts: Be the first to know about delays or disruptions.
Local Tips: Many locals prefer Moovit to other navigation apps. Join them, and you'll find yourself zipping around Barcelona like a pro.
Accessibility Options: Moovit helps find routes suitable for travelers with disabilities.
Language Support: The app supports various languages, making it traveler-friendly.

Travel Safety

Stay Safe with These Apps

AlertCops: An app to communicate with Spanish police, and report a crime or incident.
My112: Sends your location to emergency services if you call 112.
Free Wi-Fi Spots: Many plazas, parks, and public spaces in Barcelona offer free Wi-Fi. Knowing where to find them can save you data usage.
Google Maps Offline: Download the Barcelona area on Google Maps for offline navigation. Handy if you don't have a local SIM card.
Travel Adapter: Spain uses Type F electrical outlets. Having the correct adapter ensures you can charge your gadgets.
Barcelona Card: This city card provides free public transport and discounts on many attractions. You can order it online before your trip.
Taxi Booking Apps: Apps like MyTaxi can be useful if you prefer taxis to ridesharing apps like Uber.

Language Translation Apps: Google Translate or Duolingo can be helpful if you're not fluent in Spanish or Catalan. They even offer conversation mode for real-time translations.

Emergency Numbers App: Keep an app or note on your phone with emergency numbers in Barcelona, including police, medical, and consulate contact information.

Local Event Apps: Apps like TimeOut Barcelona can keep you up-to-date on local events, festivals, concerts, and more.

Restaurant Reservations: Apps like OpenTable or ElTenedor can help you reserve tables at popular restaurants in Barcelona, sometimes with exclusive discounts.

Health and Travel Insurance Apps: Have digital copies of your travel insurance, including relevant contact numbers, accessible from your phone.

Virtual Private Network (VPN): For secure browsing, especially when using public Wi-Fi spots.

Local News Apps: Stay updated on local news and regulations, especially during the uncertain times of global events or pandemics.

By embracing these technological aspects, you'll not only enhance your travel experience but also gain insights and access to local culture and conveniences. Combining these tools with the knowledge of hidden gems and day trips will set you up for an unforgettable and smooth journey in Barcelona!

Key Takeaways

- **Importance of Digital Tools:** Utilizing apps and technology can greatly enhance your travel experience in Barcelona, providing easy navigation, reservation, and exploration.
- **Money-Saving Tips:** From free Wi-Fi spots to discount cards like the Barcelona Card, there are numerous digital means to make your trip more budget-friendly.

- **Safety Precautions:** Technology also offers essential safety tools, from emergency contact apps to VPNs for secure browsing.

Action Steps

- Download offline Google Maps of Barcelona.
- Install Moovit or a similar public transportation app.
- Download a translation app such as Google Translate.
- Register for mobile payment services like Apple Pay or Venmo.
- Explore TimeOut Barcelona or other local event apps to plan your cultural immersion.
- Research and make a note of free Wi-Fi spots throughout the city.
- Familiarize yourself with the local taxi booking app or ridesharing services.

Chapter 4: A Culinary Tour of Barcelona

"First we eat, then we do everything else."
- M.F.K. Fisher

Experience Barcelona not just with your eyes, but also your taste buds. Ready to discover the true essence of this vibrant city on a plate? Grab a fork and let's dive in!

If you're thinking tapas and sangria, you're only scratching the surface of what this gastronomic haven has to offer.

In this chapter, we'll embark on a mouthwatering journey through the streets of Barcelona, exploring hidden gems that locals swear by and the iconic dishes that define the city. Whether you're a foodie on a mission or someone who just wants to spice up your travel experience, this culinary tour is meant for you.

Imagine savoring the rich flavors of seafood paella by the beach, biting into a crispy churro dipped in dark chocolate in a bustling market, or sharing a selection of tapas with newfound friends in a candlelit bodega. It's not just food; it's a feast for the senses, a cultural immersion, and a love affair with the city's very soul.

We'll also provide handy tips on dining etiquette, when and where to find the best meals, and how to order like a local. Trust me; you don't want to be that tourist who walks into a restaurant at 6 p.m. for dinner!

So, loosen your belt buckle and sharpen your appetite. It's time to eat your way through Barcelona, one tantalizing bite at a time. Ready to dig in? In the next section, we're starting with breakfast – and it's not just any old toast and coffee!

(And for those with dietary restrictions, don't worry; we have something delicious for you, too. Barcelona's culinary scene is as inclusive as it's diverse.)

Breakfast Delights

Traditional Catalan Breakfast:

Pa amb Tomàquet (Bread with Tomato):
Pa amb tomàquet is a simple yet flavorful staple in Catalan cuisine. It consists of bread rubbed with ripe tomatoes, drizzled with olive oil, and sprinkled with a touch of salt. The key to enjoying this breakfast delight is finding the freshest ingredients.

Where to find the best ones:

- **Quimet & Quimet:** A traditional bar in Poble Sec, known for its quality ingredients and authentic taste.
- **Els Quatre Gats:** An iconic spot in the Gothic Quarter that offers a cultural experience along with this classic dish.
- **Local Markets:** Don't hesitate to explore local markets like Mercat de la Boqueria, where you can grab fresh bread and tomatoes and make this dish yourself.
- **Tip:** Pair it with Spanish ham or cheese for a wholesome breakfast.

Churros and Chocolate:

Churros are deep-fried dough pastries, often enjoyed dipped in a cup of thick, rich hot chocolate. A favorite during both breakfast and snack time, churros offer a delightful crunch that perfectly complements the creamy chocolate.

Top Churrerías in the City:

- **Xurreria Banys Nous:** Located in the Barri Gòtic, this family-run xurreria has been serving traditional churros for generations.
- **Granja La Pallaresa:** A popular spot in Barri Gòtic that offers churros with both dark and milk chocolate.
- **Comaxurros:** A modern churrería in the Eixample district, known for its innovative flavors and quality chocolate.
- **Tip:** Avoid the tourist-trap locations and ask locals for their favorite churrerías. Churros are best enjoyed fresh, so look for places where they are made to order.

Local Tips:
- **Timing Matters:** Breakfast in Barcelona typically takes place a bit later than in other cultures, usually around 8-10 a.m. So take your time getting up and head to these places without the rush.
- **Experiment with Pa amb Tomàquet:** Feel free to get creative with toppings! Many local eateries will offer variations with anchovies, ham, or local cheeses.
- **Seasonal Options:** If visiting in winter, look for "porras," a thicker version of churros that's often available in cooler months.

Lunch – The Heart of the Day

Lunch is an essential part of the Spanish day, often served between 1 and 4 pm, and Barcelona's culinary landscape offers an extensive array of options to satisfy all tastes.

Tapas Galore:

Tapas are small dishes served with drinks at bars. They vary widely across Spain, and in Barcelona, you'll find a fascinating mix influenced by Catalan and Mediterranean flavors.

Traditional Tapas and Their Origin:

Patatas Bravas: Deep-fried potatoes served with spicy sauce, originating from Madrid but with unique twists in Barcelona.
Gambas al Ajillo: Garlic shrimp, a coastal favorite.
Pimientos de Padrón: Small green peppers, usually mild, fried and sprinkled with salt.

Best Tapas Bars, with Local Recommendations:

Bar Tomás: Famous for its Patatas Bravas, located in the Sarrià neighborhood.
Cervecería Catalana: A local favorite in Eixample, offering a wide variety of fresh tapas.
El Xampanyet: Historic tapas bar near the Picasso Museum, known for its atmosphere.
Tip: Don't be shy about standing at the bar, where locals often enjoy their tapas.

Seafood Paella:

Paella is one of Spain's most famous dishes, often associated with Valencia. The seafood version is particularly prominent in Barcelona due to its coastal location.

A Brief History of Paella:

Originally a meal for farmers, paella has evolved into a dish associated with celebrations and gatherings. The seafood version embraces the Mediterranean's richness.

Where to Get the Authentic Experience:

7 Portes: Established in 1836, this restaurant in Barceloneta offers a historic ambiance.
Can Solé: Another gem in Barceloneta, dating back to 1903.

Seafood Markets and Restaurants by the Beach:

La Mar Salada: Perfect for fresh seafood paella.
Mercat del Peix: Explore this market for fresh seafood and perhaps even try cooking paella yourself!
Localized Tips:
Long Lunch Culture: Remember, lunch in Barcelona is a leisurely affair. Don't be in a hurry!
Sundays and Paella: Sundays are traditional days for families to gather and enjoy paella. Join in the tradition!
Tapas Etiquette: In many tapas bars, you'll be charged based on the number of toothpicks on your plate, so keep track!

Snack Time – Merienda

Merienda is a charming Spanish tradition, a delightful pause in the afternoon to enjoy a light snack and perhaps a coffee. While the rest of

Spain may favor a sweet treat during this time, Barcelona's merienda often includes both savory and sweet options.

Empanadas and Pastries:

Empanadas:

What Are They?: Empanadas are baked or fried turnovers filled with various ingredients, such as meat, cheese, or vegetables.
Where to Try: Visit Empanadas Principe for authentic Argentine-style empanadas or Rekons, a popular spot for various empanada fillings.
Tip: These are great for on-the-go, so grab one while you're exploring the city!

Exploring Barcelona's Bakeries:

Baluard Barceloneta Bakery: Renowned for its artisan bread and pastries, this is a must-visit spot for a truly local experience.
Hoffman Pastisseria: Famous for its croissants, don't leave without trying the Mascarpone-filled one!

Sampling Catalan Pastries like 'Coca':

Coca: This is a type of flatbread commonly found in Catalonia, often sweet but also available in savory variations.
Coca de Sant Joan: If you're visiting during the Saint John's festival (June 24th), be sure to try this sweet coca topped with candied fruits.
Where to Try: Forn Mistral and Forn de Sant Jaume are popular local bakeries known for their Coca.

Local Tips:

Pair It with a Drink: Coffee or hot chocolate is a common pairing with merienda. Try a traditional Catalan "Café Bombón" - espresso with sweetened condensed milk.

Enjoy the Pace: Like all food experiences in Barcelona, merienda is meant to be leisurely. Find a nice bakery with outdoor seating and enjoy the bustling city scenes.

Festive Times: Keep an eye on local festivals as special pastries are often made to celebrate them, giving you a taste of Barcelona's rich cultural traditions.

Dinner – A Late Affair

Dinner in Barcelona is more than a meal; it's a delightful event that often begins late in the evening and may stretch into the night. Whether you prefer the grandeur of Michelin-starred restaurants or the authenticity of local eateries and bodegas, the Catalan capital has it all.

Fine Dining:

Michelin-starred Restaurants in Barcelona:

Cinc Sentits: Renowned for its innovative use of traditional Catalan ingredients. Try the tasting menu for a culinary journey.

Moments: Offering Catalan cuisine with a modern twist. The "Memory of a Morter" dish is a must-try.

Tips: Book well in advance, and don't hesitate to ask for wine pairings. Dress to impress!

Signature Dishes to Try:

Suquet de Peix: A Catalan fish stew available at many fine dining establishments.

Canelons: Often served on St. Stephen's Day, these stuffed pasta rolls are a Catalan delight.

Local Eateries and Bodegas:

1. Recommendations for Neighborhood Favorites:

Bar Tomas: Famous for its Patatas Bravas, a staple tapa dish in Barcelona.

La Cova Fumada: Known for "Bombas," spicy meat-stuffed potato balls. A real hidden gem!

2. Vegetarian and Vegan Dinner Spots:

Rasoterra: A vegetarian bistro that offers locally sourced dishes. Their tasting menu caters to vegans too.

Cat Bar: A fully vegan burger and craft beer spot. Try the "Black Cat" burger!

Localized Tips:

Dine Late: Dinner in Barcelona often starts after 9 PM. Embrace the local dining schedule for a genuine experience.

Ask the Locals: Don't be shy to ask for recommendations; locals love sharing their favorite spots.

Consider a Vermouth: Many locals start their dinner with a glass of vermouth. Join in this tradition at a local bodega.

Sweets and Desserts

If you've saved room for dessert, Barcelona has a sweet treat waiting just for you. From traditional Crema Catalana to artisanal ice cream, indulging in Catalan confections is a must-do for every food enthusiast. Here's where you can treat your sweet tooth:

Crema Catalana:

Crema Catalana, often referred to as Catalonia's crème brûlée, is a rich custard dessert topped with caramelized sugar. This delectable treat embodies the essence of Catalan cuisine.

Where to find this local favorite:

Can Culleretes: Established in 1786, this place serves one of the most authentic Crema Catalana in Barcelona.
Els Quatre Gats: A historic café and restaurant, famous for its artistic connections and delicious desserts.
Tips: Pair Crema Catalana with a local sweet wine like Moscatell for an unforgettable dessert experience.

Artisanal Ice Cream Shops:

Barcelona's warm weather invites you to explore its vibrant ice cream scene, filled with unique flavors and seasonal offerings.

A guide to unique flavors and seasonal treats:

Gelaaati! Di Marco: Known for its selection of dairy-free and gluten-free options, along with classic flavors.
Parallelo: If you're seeking adventurous flavors like saffron or olive oil, this is the place to go.
Eyescream and Friends: For Instagram-worthy servings and exotic combinations, don't miss this spot.
Tips: Look out for seasonal offerings such as fresh fig or citrus-based ice creams during the summer months.

Localized Tips:

Explore Local Flavors: Apart from the classics, try some unique Catalan flavors such as turrón (almond nougat) or rosemary honey.

Embrace the Season: Many ice cream shops offer seasonal flavors, reflecting the local produce of the region. Ask for recommendations.

Drinks and Nightlife

When the sun sets, Barcelona's nightlife comes alive, offering a world of flavors, from traditional sangria and cava to inventive cocktails. Whether you're a wine connoisseur or a cocktail enthusiast, Barcelona's bars, clubs, and wineries offer a splash of local culture that's not to be missed.

Sangria and Cava:

Sangria, the fruity wine punch, and cava, Catalonia's sparkling wine, are must-try beverages that encapsulate the essence of Spanish festivity.

Traditional beverage spots:

Bodega la Palma: A classic spot for sangria with a local feel.
Can Paixano (La Xampanyeria): A legendary cava bar serving up bubbly goodness with delicious tapas.
Tips: Join a cava tasting tour to learn about the traditional method of making sparkling wine, used in Catalonia.

Local wine and cava tastings:

Vila Viniteca: An excellent wine shop offering tasting sessions and classes.
Recaredo: Visit this family-run winery for an intimate cava tasting experience.
Cavas Freixenet: Offers tours and tastings in one of Spain's most renowned cava producers.

Cocktail Bars and Nightlife:

Barcelona's nightlife is as varied as its culinary scene. From sleek rooftop bars to hidden speakeasies, the city offers something for every palate.

Best places for cocktails:

Dry Martini: A classic cocktail bar renowned for its martinis and elegant atmosphere.
Paradiso: A hidden gem behind a pastrami shop, this speakeasy serves innovative cocktails.
Eclipse Barcelona: For a luxurious experience, enjoy cocktails at this rooftop bar with panoramic city views.
Macera TallerBar: If you're after craft cocktails with house-made spirits, don't miss this spot.
Tips: Many bars offer a daily happy hour with special discounts, usually between 6-8 p.m.
Localized Tips:
Know the Time: Spaniards tend to dine and drink late. Don't be surprised to find bars bustling well past midnight.
Explore the Neighborhoods: Different neighborhoods offer diverse nightlife experiences. The Gothic Quarter is rich in history, while El Born is known for trendy bars.
Ask the Locals: Often, the best spots are known only to the locals. Don't hesitate to ask for recommendations.
Drink Responsibly: With so much to explore, it's easy to get carried away. Enjoy the flavors and the night, but always drink responsibly.

Nightlife Guide: Extend Your Evening in Barcelona

Barcelona's nightlife is as effervescent as its culture. The city that never sleeps offers an array of experiences for night owls. From upscale clubs to local hangouts, the night can be as wild or as serene as you like.

Clubs and Dance Venues:

1. Pacha Barcelona:

Address: Passeig Marítim, 38, 08003 Barcelona
How to Get There: Metro L4 (Ciutadella | Vila Olímpica). Safe area but always be cautious at late hours.
What to Expect: Iconic Ibiza vibes, international DJs.

2. Shôko Barcelona:

Address: Passeig Marítim, 36, 08003 Barcelona
How to Get There: Metro L4 (Ciutadella | Vila Olímpica). Well-lit area with ample transportation.
What to Expect: A fusion of restaurant and club; transforms into a dance venue at night.

3. Macarena Club:

Address: Carrer Nou de Sant Francesc, 5, 08002 Barcelona
How to Get There: Metro L3 (Drassanes). Central location, follow usual city safety protocols.
What to Expect: An intimate club experience with electronic music.

Jazz and Live Music

1. Harlem Jazz Club:

Address: Carrer de Comtessa de Sobradiel, 8, 08002 Barcelona
How to Get There: Metro L3 (Liceu). Busy area, good for nighttime strolls.
What to Expect: A jazz institution with a multicultural vibe.

2. Jamboree:

Address: Plaça Reial, 17, 08002 Barcelona
How to Get There: Metro L3 (Liceu). Located in a popular square with taxis available.
What to Expect: Legendary jazz and hip-hop performances.

Rooftop Bars

Sky Bar at Grand Hotel Central:

Address: Via Laietana, 30, 08003 Barcelona
How to Get There: Metro L4 (Jaume I). Upscale area, known to be safe.
What to Expect: Panoramic views and chic cocktails.

Localized Tips:

Dress Code: Many clubs enforce a dress code. Smart casual is usually safe.
Entrance Fees: Check in advance if there are entrance fees or if you need to be on a guest list.
Safety First: Like any city, keep your belongings close and use trusted transportation methods.
Last Metro: Keep in mind the metro's closing time if you plan on using it to return.
Use Reliable Apps: Taxi apps like "MyTaxi" can ensure a safe ride back.

Language: A simple "Hola" and "Gracias" can go a long way. Most staff speak English, but local etiquette is appreciated.
Cultural Sensitivity: Be mindful of local customs and behavior. Whether dancing the night away or enjoying a relaxed evening with live music, Barcelona's nightlife promises a memorable experience. Always remember to prioritize your safety and well-being, follow local guidance, and, most importantly, have fun! Barcelona's night awaits you!

Key Takeaways

- **Breakfast Delights:** Pa amb tomàquet and churros with chocolate are not to be missed.
- **Lunch – The Heart of the Day:** Tapas and seafood paella are essential culinary experiences.
- **Snack Time – Merienda:** Try local bakeries for empanadas and 'Coca.'
- **Dinner – A Late Affair:** Whether fine dining or local eateries, dinner in Barcelona is a sensory feast.
- **Sweets and Desserts:** Indulge in Crema Catalana and artisanal ice creams.
- **Drinks and Nightlife:** Savor traditional beverages like Sangria and Cava, and explore the vibrant nightlife.

Action Steps

- **Make Reservations:** Some popular restaurants may require reservations, especially during peak times.
- **Dietary Restrictions:** Inform the restaurant of any dietary needs in advance.
- **Local Etiquette:** Understanding local dining customs can enhance your experience.

- **Avoid Tourist Traps:** Seek local recommendations or use trusted apps for genuine culinary experiences.
- **Seasonal Delights:** Ask for seasonal or daily specials to enjoy fresh, local produce.
- **Language Barrier:** Having a translation app or a small phrasebook might be handy.
- **Reservations:** Apps like OpenTable or contacting the restaurant directly can secure your spot.
- **Avoiding Peak Times:** If you prefer a quieter dining experience, ask locals for the best times to dine.
- **Street Food Caution:** Enjoy street food from reputable vendors to avoid any health concerns.
- **Tipping Practices:** Tipping is not customary in Spain but is appreciated for good service.

Embark on a culinary journey that's as rich and flavorful as Barcelona itself. Happy eating, and "Bon Profit!" (Enjoy your meal!)

Conclusion

Barcelona, a city that pulsates with life, energy, and culture, offers far more than the glittering façades of its well-known attractions. As we've explored throughout this book, the magic of Barcelona lies not only in its grand monuments but also in its hidden alleys, the vast landscapes beyond the city, and the flavors of its rich culinary tradition.

Main Takeaways:

The Value of Venturing into Lesser-Known Territories: From the artistic charm of El Poblenou to the tranquil maze of Laberint d'Horta, Barcelona's hidden gems unveil a world away from the tourist-packed mainstays.

The Beauty that Lies in Neighboring Towns and Cities: Day trips to Montserrat, Sitges, and Girona demonstrate that Barcelona's enchantment extends far beyond its city limits.

Embracing Modern Technology to Enhance Travel Experiences: The integration of mobile payments, transportation apps, and safety tools not only simplifies but elevates the travel experience.

The Magic that Unfolds When You Attempt to Speak Like a Local: Whether it's ordering paella in Catalan or negotiating at Mercat de la Boqueria, communicating in the local language adds authenticity to the journey.

Barcelona is not a destination to merely visit; it's a city to experience, to immerse oneself in, to taste, hear, and feel. It's a place where every street has a history, every dish tells a tale, and every adventure is an invitation to discover something new.

Get out there! Barcelona awaits your unique journey. Whether you're an art enthusiast, a food lover, a tech-savvy traveler, or someone looking to explore beyond the beaten path, this city has something special for you. And as you traverse its vibrant streets, remember, every step is a story waiting to be told. Don't just travel; live Barcelona. Let your feet wander, let your taste buds explore, and let your heart fall in love with the essence of this extraordinary city.

BOOK 3

Valencia Travel Guide

Explore to Win

Introduction

"Travel makes one modest, you see what a tiny place you occupy in the world."
— Gustave Flaubert

Ever packed your suitcase, excited for a trip, only to end up in the same tourist-packed spots as every other traveler clutching a guidebook? Well, buckle up, dear reader, because Valencia is calling, and it's not interested in clichés.

You want to taste the real paella, not the microwaved version in a pan. You yearn to explore the narrow alleys without bumping into selfie sticks at every corner. You desire the Spanish experience, not the "made for tourists" souvenir package. In short, you're in a pickle, and this book is your fork. Yes, you read that right, a fork, because food is a serious business in Valencia, and so is having fun.

Think of this guide as a quirky local buddy who knows Valencia inside and out. He's (the book's a 'he' now, roll with it) going to show you around the town, crack a few jokes, and make sure you're stuffed with all the local food you can handle. Best part? No need to buy him a drink at the end of the night.

See, while there are countless travel guides that take you through the splendid sights and sounds of Valencia, this one's a bit different. It doesn't just stop at showing you the landmarks and well-known eateries; it nudges you to explore, to taste, to feel Valencia in a way that's uniquely yours.

Imagine yourself sipping horchata in a tucked-away spot only the locals know about or meandering through a vibrant market that's not splashed all over every travel site. Sounds refreshing, doesn't it?

This book is inspired by my love for Valencia and a belief that every traveler deserves an experience that resonates with their unique taste. From the bustling streets to the tranquil parks, Valencia has a rhythm of its own, and I'm here to help you dance to it.

Me? I am just a humble explorer with a passion for authentic experiences, local food, and sharing the secrets of a city I've fallen head over heels for. Valencia has captured my heart, and now it's my mission to make sure it captures yours, without the tourist traps, of course.

From the sun-kissed beaches to the late-night churro stands, Valencia is more than just another Spanish city; it's an adventure waiting to happen. And don't worry, there won't be any "visit this famous landmark because everyone does" here. We're diving deep, and we're diving locally.

We'll surely visit the must-see sites, for they are majestic and full of history, but we'll do it with a twist, adding layers of understanding, context, and local perspective that make these places come alive in a whole new light.

This book is for those who want to dive a little deeper, to get a taste of Valencia that goes beyond the surface, to create memories that are uniquely theirs. It's not just about seeing the sights; it's about feeling the pulse of Valencia, understanding its soul, and leaving with a piece of it carved in your heart.

Prepare to start your journey into the hidden alleyways and secret recipes of Valencia. You'll laugh, you'll eat, you'll dance, and who knows, you might even learn a thing or two. Ready to break the tourist mold? Valencia's ready for you. So, turn the page, and let's begin this adventure, shall we?

Chapter 1: Valencia – The Heart of the Mediterranean

"Spain is not a country, it's a world."
- Béla Bartók.

Valencia! The Heart of the Mediterranean, the Land of Paella, and a city that's been waiting for someone as adventurous and charming as you. Yes, you! No need to look over your shoulder.

It's time to peel back the citrus-scented layers of this wonderful city and uncover the juicy details that make it a destination you'll never forget.

Now, I know what you're thinking: "Another history lesson? Yawn!" But trust me, Valencia's history is more thrilling than a telenovela marathon, and it's got plot twists that'll make your head spin. From Romans and Moors to the epic architectural marvels of Santiago Calatrava, Valencia has seen it all and lived to tell the tale.

And the culture! It's not just a series of museums and fancy words; it's a living, breathing, dance-till-you-drop experience that you'll want to soak in with all your senses.

So, grab your metaphorical Matador's cape (or a real one if you're feeling snazzy), because we're about to charge headfirst into Valencia's rich history, quirky customs, unique identity, and yes, the food that'll make you want to write sonnets.

In this chapter, we'll explore:

- Valencia's intriguing origins, complete with battles, love stories, and architectural wonders.
- The unique Valencian identity that defies stereotypes and revels in its diversity.
- The cultures and traditions that are as vibrant as a Fallas firecracker.

Whether you're a history buff or someone who thinks the Renaissance was a hotel chain, there's something here that'll tickle your fancy.

Shall we?

A City Born from Battles

First things first: Romans! You know, those folks who gave us roads, aqueducts, and toga parties. They founded Valencia in 138 BC, naming it "Valentia," which means 'strength' or 'valor.' How's that for an impressive start?

Now, if you think that's all, you've clearly never studied Spanish history. The Moors arrived in the 8th century and transformed Valencia into a cultural and commercial hub, leaving behind splendid architectural marvels.

Love in the Time of Reconquista

Remember El Cid? No, not the Amazon Prime series, but the real legendary knight! He took over Valencia from the Moors in a tale filled with battles, intrigue, and romance. They say he rode his horse into battle with his deceased wife by his side to rally the troops. Now, that's commitment!

Architectural Wonders to Swoon Over

Valencia's architecture isn't just a feast for the eyes; it's an all-you-can-eat buffet of styles and periods. From the Gothic glory of the Cathedral to the futuristic marvel of the City of Arts and Sciences, Valencia will woo you with its architectural charm.

The Silk Exchange (La Lonja) is so dazzling that UNESCO had no choice but to call it a World Heritage Site. And let's not forget the medieval charm of the Torres de Serranos, which once stood as grand gateways to the city.

Modern Twists and Turns

Valencia hasn't rested on its historical laurels. The Turia Gardens, once a flood-prone river, is now a 9-kilometer stretch of lush parkland, making the city an urban planner's dream. Talk about a plot twist!

The beauty of Valencia's history is that it's not trapped behind glass in some stuffy museum. It's alive in every cobblestone street, in the echoes of the Fallas festival, and in the savory scent of paella wafting through the air.

So, there you have it, the intricate tapestry of Valencia's origins, served with a side of enthusiasm and a sprinkling of wit.

Language: More Than Just Spanish

Hold onto your language books! Did you know that Valencians speak a language all their own? It's called Valencian, and it's a variety of the Catalan language. While you'll certainly hear Spanish spoken, the Valencian tongue adds a local flavor. Think of it as linguistic salsa on your travel taco.

Cuisine: Paella and Beyond

Here's a fun fact: paella, the rice dish that's as synonymous with Spain as, well, sangria, originates from Valencia. But don't you dare ask for

"Spanish paella"; around these parts, it's Valencian paella! And the locals are rightfully proud of this saffron-infused marvel.

But Valencian cuisine is more than just a one-hit wonder. Dive into the world of fideuà (noodle paella), horchata (a refreshing milky beverage), and an endless array of market-fresh seafood. Your taste buds will thank you.

Festivals: Fallas, Fire, and Fun

If you think festivals are just about parades and music, Valencia is about to rewrite the rulebook. Take the Fallas Festival, a riotous celebration of fire, artistry, and, let's face it, noise. Giant sculptures (fallas) are crafted, displayed, and then set ablaze in a spectacular bonfire. It's like Mardi Gras met Burning Man, and they decided to throw a party in Valencia.

Arts and Music

Valencia's arts scene is as varied and vibrant as a kaleidoscope. From street art that turns ordinary walls into canvases to the Palau de la Música's top-notch classical performances, Valencia's creative spirit is inescapable. Ever watched an opera in an architectural marvel? The Queen Sofia Palace of the Arts offers that opportunity.

Sports and Recreation

Sure, Valencians love their football, but have you heard of pilota? It's a traditional Valencian ball game, and it's a blast to watch. Add to that the city's passion for cycling, water sports, and running, and you've got a city that loves to play as hard as it works.

In Valencia, diversity isn't a buzzword; it's a way of life. It's in the languages spoken, the dishes savored, the festivals celebrated, and even the sports played. This city defies stereotypes, embraces its quirks, and invites you to do the same.

The Blend Between Traditional and Modern Valencia

You know that friend who somehow manages to be both the life of the party and the wise sage, depending on the occasion? Meet Valencia. A city where the history blends seamlessly with a forward-thinking modernity. It's like your grandpa rocking out to the latest hits – a surprise that somehow works beautifully.

A Tale of Two Cities? Not Quite. Valencia doesn't just mix the old with the new; it blends them into a delightful cocktail that leaves you pleasantly tipsy. It's like your hip grandma who wears vintage pearls with her trendy sneakers - effortlessly cool and never boring.

Old School Charm

In the historic heart of the city, you'll find Valencia Cathedral, a Gothic beauty with a little Romanesque and Baroque sprinkled in, just because. Climb the Miguelete Tower and reward yourself with views that stretch as far as your Spanish vocabulary. Then, descend and lose yourself in the winding lanes of El Carmen, where every turn uncovers a charming square, a local bar, or a boutique that you never knew you needed to visit.

Got a taste for the truly traditional? Head to the Mercado Central, where Valencians have shopped for fresh produce, meats, and spices since 1928. It's like stepping into a foodie's dream, only the dream is real, and it smells like jamón.

Modern Magic

But Valencia isn't just content to rest on its historical laurels. Stroll down to the City of Arts and Sciences, and you'll think you've just walked onto a sci-fi movie set. Designed by the famed architect Santiago Calatrava, this futuristic complex is part science museum, part opera house, part aquarium, and entirely awesome.

Even the beaches have gotten in on the act. Once the haunt of fishermen, today's Valencia beachfront is a vibrant mix of boardwalk cafes, modernist buildings, and an endless stretch of golden sand.

A Harmony Like No Other
What makes Valencia truly special is how it harmonizes these contrasting elements. The futuristic doesn't overshadow the historic; it complements it. It's a city where you can enjoy a traditional Valencian paella for lunch and then catch an opera in a spaceship-like building for dinner.

And let's not forget the festivals. From the traditional Fallas Festival, complete with its larger-than-life sculptures and fireworks, to modern music festivals that draw international crowds, Valencia has mastered the art of partying in every era.

So, dear reader, ready to take a leap through time? In Valencia, every step can take you from the centuries-old to the cutting-edge, often in the same block. It's a city that defies categorization, that loves its traditions but isn't afraid to embrace the new. It's what makes Valencia unique, enchanting, and unmissable.

Key Takeaways

- **Historical Harmony:** Valencia's unique blend of historical and modern architecture offers a timeless appeal, evident in landmarks like Valencia Cathedral and the City of Arts and Sciences.
- **Cultural Richness:** From traditional markets to futuristic museums, Valencia's cultural landscape is diverse, reflecting both its rich history and innovative spirit.

- **Dynamic Festivities:** Valencia is home to a range of festivals, like the Fallas Festival, that celebrate both traditional and contemporary aspects of its culture.
- **Culinary Traditions:** The city's culinary scene, including its famous paella, showcases a blend of time-honored recipes and modern gastronomy.
- **Beaches and Boardwalks:** Valencia's beachfront combines traditional charm with modern amenities, offering a vibrant coastal experience.
- **Unified Contrasts:** Valencia's real magic lies in its ability to unify contrasts, making old and new elements complement rather than compete with each other, offering a truly unique travel experience.

Action Steps

- **Explore Historical Sites:** Plan a visit to both the historic Valencia Cathedral and the modern City of Arts and Sciences to witness the architectural harmony.
- **Attend a Local Festival:** If visiting during the Fallas Festival, don't miss out on this unique cultural experience; book tickets and accommodations early.
- **Try Traditional Cuisine:** Schedule a traditional Valencian meal, particularly paella at a reputable local restaurant. Seek recommendations or check out online reviews.
- **Walk the Beaches:** Spend an afternoon exploring the boardwalk and beaches, soaking in both the traditional charm and modern amenities.
- **Visit a Local Market:** Take time to explore a traditional market like Mercado Central to experience local life, tastes, and crafts.

- **Capture the Contrast:** Bring a camera to document the unique blend of old and new in Valencia's urban landscape; these memories will last a lifetime.
- **Join a Guided Tour:** If available, consider a guided tour that focuses on Valencia's historical and modern blend; local guides often offer insights that you won't find in typical travel literature.

Chapter 2: Iconic Landmarks and Must-Visit Attractions

"Spain is a fascinating mix of people, languages, culture, and food, but if there is one thing all Spaniards share, it's a love for life."
- José Andrés.

If you've ever found yourself daydreaming about the sultry Mediterranean breeze caressing your face as you gaze upon architectural marvels that make you question your own doodling abilities, then buckle up, my friend! You're in for a Valencian ride that's more thrilling than a paella-cooking contest judged by your Spanish grandma.

In this chapter, we're not just visiting the postcard favorites, but delving into the soul of Valencia through its landmarks. Think of the City of Arts and Sciences as a futuristic playground designed by an architect with a sci-fi addiction, or the Silk Exchange, which looks like it's been lifted straight out of a fairy tale (complete with potential dragons hiding in the basement).

"But what's the catch?" you ask. No catch, just a cautionary tale: If you're planning to whip out the 'been-there-done-that' attitude, prepare to be humbled. Valencia's landmarks are more multifaceted than a mystery novel penned by an over-caffeinated writer.

Valencia's iconic landmarks are calling, and trust me, you'll want to answer!

Plaza de Toros de València

Welcome to the Plaza de Toros de València, where passion, drama, and heritage come together in a grand amphitheater. It was built in 1859, this monumental structure echoes the Colosseum in Rome. The neoclassical architecture alone is enough to make your jaw drop like you've just bitten into a particularly zesty piece of citrus. It's round, robust, and regal - a real architectural marvel that can seat up to 12,000 spectators.

But it's not all about what meets the eye. The essence of this place lies in the bullfighting tradition. Whether or not you're a fan of the sport, understanding it is akin to peeking through a keyhole into the Spanish soul.
But hey, let's not forget the practicalities:

Getting there: Metro lines 3 and 7. Hop off at Xàtiva station, and you're there.
Tickets: Depending on the event, prices may vary. It's best to check online or at the ticket booth.
Food: You're in the heart of Valencia, so food options are aplenty. Try a local eatery nearby for some post-bullfight tapas.
Best time to visit: Bullfighting season mainly runs from March to October, but the arena and museum are accessible year-round.

Plaza de la Reina

Plaza de la Reina in Valencia is not just a square; it's an open-air theater where life plays out. Picture yourself stepping into a vibrant space, greeted by the grand fountain, surrounded by historical buildings and swaying palm trees. A quick glance, and you'll find the majestic Valencia Cathedral, which we'll dive deeper into.

Wander around, and you're part of a colorful painting—artists sketching, lovers stealing kisses, and children laughing. Sip an Agua de Valencia at a café and let the symphony of local life serenade you.

Getting there: Follow the buzz or hop on bus lines 62, 70, 71, 73, C1.
Tickets: Just your presence.
Food: A myriad of tapas bars awaits.
Best time to visit: Early mornings and late afternoons.

City of Arts and Sciences (Ciudad de las Artes y las Ciencias)

City of Arts and Sciences, or as the locals call it, "Ciudad de las Artes y las Ciencias." A place where Salvador Dali and Star Trek had a baby, and that baby decided to settle down by a futuristic lagoon. Yes, it's as mind-blowing as it sounds.

Now, what exactly is this sci-fi wonderland? It's a complex dedicated to promoting human intelligence and culture, sprawled across an area that's so vast, that you'd need a spaceship to see it all in a day. Designed by the world-renowned architect Santiago Calatrava, this place isn't just a feast for the eyes; it's a buffet for the brain.

There's the Hemisfèric, where you can explore the cosmos through its planetarium or dive into the deep blue through its IMAX cinema. The Opera House, shaped like a gigantic helmet (or a sci-fi beetle, depending on how many sangrias you've had), offers cultural performances that can make even the stiffest opera-haters tap their feet.

Don't forget the Science Museum, where 'Do Not Touch' signs are replaced by 'Please Poke This.' It's science made fun, and you can even launch a water rocket or watch your own skeleton ride a bicycle.

Practical Tips

Getting There: Take Bus Line 95 or Tram Line 4; it's as easy as pie.
Tickets: Many parts are free to access; for others, a combo ticket is available.
Food: On-site restaurants or pack a picnic, your choice!
Footwear: Comfy shoes are a must; it's a vast place.
Best Time to Visit: Early morning or late afternoon to dodge those crowds.
Language Tip: Practice 'Ciudad de las Artes y las Ciencias' in the mirror before you go, and impress the locals.

Now, you're armed with all you need to explore Valencia's futuristic marvel without getting lost, hungry, or footsore! Happy exploring!

Valencia Cathedral

Valencia Cathedral, or La Seu, is like that mysterious friend who's lived many lives and seen many things. This beautiful piece of architecture is just so full of history and, quite frankly, personality. It's like an old wise elder sitting in the heart of the city, holding stories that span over centuries. Gothic, Romanesque, and Baroque architectural styles all decided to have a party, and Valencia Cathedral was born. And guess what? It supposedly houses the real Holy Grail. Yep, the one and only!

Whether you're a history buff, architecture lover, or just plain old curious, Valencia Cathedral has a place for you. It's not just a building; it's a storybook, each stone whispering tales of the past.

And to make sure you don't spend your entire vacation just finding the place, here's a cheat sheet:
Getting There: Hop on Bus Lines 4, 5, 9, 16, or 28; it's like a big city wide web leading to the spider (in this case, a beautiful cathedral).

Tickets: Small fee for adults; kids might just get in on the house (check for seasonal changes).
Food: Nearby cafes abound with local flavors; try a Valencia orange, it's the citrusy law.
Best Time to Visit: Weekdays in the morning to avoid the tourist hordes.
Footwear: Something walkable; there's exploring to be done.
Fun Tip: Don't miss the Miguelete Tower; the views are, quite literally, top-notch.

Valencia Cathedral isn't just a spot on a map; it's a journey into the heart and soul of Valencia. Pack your sense of wonder (and good shoes) and prepare for a date with history!

Central Market (Mercado Central)

When your taste buds demand a party, and your inner foodie screams for an adventure, Valencia's Central Market is the ultimate destination. This gastronomic palace, with its stunning Modernist architecture, hosts a culinary celebration every day (except Sundays, because even markets need a siesta).

From succulent Spanish meats to cheeses that would make a mouse's dream come true, Mercado Central is where Valencia's flavors strut their stuff. It's not just a place to buy food; it's a sensory overload, an experience that turns shopping into an exotic dance of sights, smells, and tastes.

Now, for the nuts and bolts:

Getting There: Metro Lines 1 and 5 are your chariots. Follow the wafting aroma of paella.
Tickets: No entry fee but brace your wallet for the tantalizing temptations within.

Food: Try a refreshing horchata paired with fartons. And no, that's not a type of medieval weapon; it's a delicious local treat.

Best Time to Visit: Mornings are your golden ticket to freshness. Late afternoons? Not so much.

Bargaining Skills: Channel your inner merchant, and you might snag a deal. Or at least a smile.

So, grab your reusable bags and your appetite, and wander through a maze where every turn uncovers a new delicacy. Central Market is not a pit stop; it's an epicurean journey. But beware, the aisles are paved with culinary temptation; resistance is, as they say, futile!

The Silk Exchange (La Lonja de la Seda)

If walls could whisper, La Lonja de la Seda would weave tales of merchants, silks, and grandeur in Valencia's golden age. This UNESCO World Heritage site is an architectural gem that displays the opulence and power of the city's mercantile days. With its intricate stonework and majestic columns resembling twisted rope, the Silk Exchange is no mere building; it's a homage to the splendor of commerce.

Back in the day, traders would swagger around the main hall, flicking coins and cracking deals. Today, La Lonja lets you traverse time, stepping into a world where art met economics, and where the fine lines of Gothic architecture were as impressive as the silks traded within. Yes, friends, it's not just a building; it's a standing ovation to history.

Now, let's get down to the brass tacks:

Getting There: Hop on Bus 4, 7, or 27. Or simply follow the trail of awestruck tourists.

Tickets: Your wallet can relax; it's free on Sundays and public holidays.

Food: Fancy some gourmet silk? Kidding! For edibles, explore nearby cafes.

Best Time to Visit: Early morning for serenity, late afternoon for golden hues on the stone.

Photography Skills: Bring them. This place is Instagram's fairy godmother.

La Lonja de la Seda is a flirtation with the past, a wink to the extraordinary, and a salute to human ingenuity. Whether you're a lover of history, architecture, or simply enjoy standing in awe of beautiful things, this slice of the past is a feast for the eyes. And hey, it's even got a gargoyles' court – who wouldn't want to chat with a stone dragon?

Oceanogràfic

Dive into a world of underwater wonders without even getting wet at Valencia's Oceanogràfic. Housed in the jaw-dropping City of Arts and Sciences complex, this place is the largest aquarium in Europe. But who's counting square feet when you've got beluga whales waving at you?

Oceanogràfic is like that friend who knows a guy everywhere. From arctic penguins to tropical jellyfish, it's a who's who of the marine kingdom. It doesn't just display fish; it serves as a watery stage for dolphins to perform ballet, sharks to glide menacingly, and sea lions to impersonate your uncle at a family gathering.

Designed by Félix Candela, the avant-garde architecture itself mimics the grace of marine life. Picture walking through underwater tunnels as sharks loom overhead or watching rainbow colors in the Jellyfish Gallery.

It's a world beneath the waves, with no snorkeling gear required.

Ready to set sail? Here's your captain's log:

Getting There: Bus lines 99, 95. No, swimming is not an option.
Tickets: Not free, but the memories are priceless. Check the website for the prices.
Food: Hungry? The underwater restaurant lets you dine with fish. Or, for quick bites, kiosks are scattered around.
Best Time to Visit: Late afternoon when the sun and crowds have mellowed.
Don't Forget: A camera, curiosity, and your inner child.

Oceanogràfic is more than a splashy tourist attraction. It's a space that celebrates the diversity and beauty of our oceans. If you've ever wondered how a walrus yawns or what a dolphin's laugh sounds like, this is the place to find out. You don't need a boat, just a ticket, and a sense of wonder. Now, who's up for meeting Nemo?

Turia Gardens (Jardín del Turia)

Turia Gardens is what happens when a city takes lemons and makes the most astonishing lemonade. A devastating flood in 1957 led Valencia to reroute the Turia River, leaving a dry riverbed. But instead of turning it into a concrete nightmare, the Valencians turned it into a 9-kilometer-long garden. Talk about urban transformation goals!

Imagine strolling down a river without a drop of water in sight. In Turia Gardens, you'll find everything from playgrounds to sports facilities, fountains, sculptures, and even an opera house. And no, you don't need a boat. It's like Central Park, but with a Spanish flair, minus the river part. It's your morning jog spot, your romantic evening walk, your picnicking with friends' venue, all rolled into one.

What's that? You want to jog, cycle, and maybe take up tai chi? Well, dust off your running shoes, oil that bike chain, and limber up. Turia Gardens is your go-to spot. You'll be among trees, flowers, birds, and if you're lucky, maybe a free concert or two.

Now, here's your explorer's kit:

Getting There: Bus lines 13, 14, 25, 95 or Train line C3. If you can't find it, just follow the locals on bicycles.
Tickets: Free as the breeze through the orange trees.
Food: Pack a picnic or grab a coffee at one of the kiosks, but don't feed the birds; they're on a diet.
Best Time to Visit: Early morning or late afternoon to catch the glow and the flow of Valencia's finest green space.

Bioparc Valencia

Bioparc Valencia is the wild heart of the city, and by wild, I mean the kind of place where you can stare into the eyes of a gorilla one minute and the next, stand face-to-face with a hungry crocodile. It's like a safari without the long flight to Africa. Curious? Read on!

This innovative zoo uses a "zoo-immersion" concept that ditches the cages and creates environments that replicate the natural habitats of the animals. From the lush wetlands of Equatorial Africa to the arid landscapes of Madagascar, you can travel continents within a few footsteps. The animals seem to be more at home here, and it's not uncommon to catch an intimate moment of their daily lives. Don't be surprised if you see elephants playing in the water or lemurs leaping right over your head.

Bioparc Valencia isn't merely a feast for the eyes but an ethical step towards responsible tourism. The park plays an active role in conservation efforts and is a center for education about the environment. Ready for your safari within the city? Here's what you need to know:

Getting There: Bus lines 95, 98, 99, or the metro to Nou d'Octubre station. You can't miss the giant elephants at the entrance!
Tickets: Not free, but a reasonable charge considering the wild ride you're in for. Discounts are available for kids and seniors.
Food: Cafes offer food for humans, not elephants. Though sharing with a giraffe would make a great story!
Best Time to Visit: Weekdays, early morning or late afternoon, to avoid crowds and catch feeding times.
What to Wear: Your best safari chic, of course! Or, you know, just comfortable walking shoes.

Bioparc Valencia breaks the mold of traditional zoos and invites you on a wild adventure that respects both the creatures it houses and the world they hail from. You're not just visiting a zoo; you're taking a step into the wild itself. Just remember, the crocodiles are not up for selfies, no matter how much they smile!

L'Almoina Archaeological Center

L'Almoina Archaeological Center in Valencia is where time travel becomes a reality. No, you don't need a DeLorean, just a curiosity for the ancient world! Nestled in the heart of the city, this historical hub invites you on a journey to the roots of Valencia, and it doesn't even require a flux capacitor!

What might look like an unassuming building from the outside houses a wealth of history. L'Almoina showcases Valencia's ancient ruins, revealing layers of history, from the Roman city of Valentia, founded in 138 BC, to the Visigoths and Moors that left their marks over the centuries. You'll discover baths, roads, houses, and even parts of the ancient city wall. Every stone tells a story of wars, empires, and daily life from millennia ago.

L'Almoina is more than a collection of relics; it's a living narrative of Valencia's past. Through interactive exhibits, meticulous reconstructions, and informative displays, you'll get a sense of what life was like in the different eras. You'll walk on the same roads that Roman citizens once strolled and discover secrets that only time can tell.

Ready to embark on this historical adventure? Here's what you need to know:

Getting There: Bus lines 115, 25, 95, C2 or Tram lines 4 and 6 to Alameda station, then a scenic walk to the old city.
Tickets: Free. No need to barter like an ancient merchant.
Food: You might not find Roman feasts, but local eateries serve delicious modern Valencian dishes.
Best Time to Visit: Early morning or late afternoon to enjoy the site without the bustling crowds.

L'Almoina Archaeological Center is your gateway to Valencia's rich history. Forget your history textbooks; this is where the past comes to life. Whether you're a history buff or just someone looking for an extraordinary experience, L'Almoina offers a peek into a world long gone, yet still alive beneath our feet. Just don't tell anyone I offered you a ride in my time-traveling DeLorean, deal?

Key Takeaways

- **City of Arts and Sciences:** modern architectural marvel with a blend of culture, arts, and science; easy to reach, best explored in early morning or late afternoon.

- **Valencia Cathedral**: Visit this iconic cathedral early morning or late afternoon to witness a historical marvel housing the Holy Grail.
- **Central Market:** Dive into local flavors and bustle at this early-opening market.
- The Silk Exchange: Step into Valencia's trade history at this UNESCO site; best visited in the morning.
- **Oceanogràfic:** Explore Europe's largest aquarium with over 500 species.
- **Turia Gardens:** Enjoy leisure time in this unique park in a dried riverbed; free and open 24/7.
- **Bioparc Valencia:** Experience an immersive African safari-like zoo.
- **L'Almoina Archaeological Center:** Journey through ancient Valencia from Roman to Moorish times.

Action Steps

- **Plan Your Route:** Valencia's attractions are spread out; plan a route that groups nearby sites together, and utilize local transport like bikes or trams.
- **Embrace Local Cuisine:** Look for locally recommended eateries and ask for daily specials, especially near the Central Market. Try horchata with fartons, a Valencian specialty.
- **Seek Local Events:** Check community boards or local websites for festivals, exhibitions, or free entry days to cultural sites like L'Almoina Archaeological Center.
- **Connect with a Local Guide:** Hire a local guide for at least one day. Their insights into places like The Silk Exchange will enrich your experience.
- **Pack for Adventure and Leisure:** With outdoor spots like Turia Gardens and fascinating venues like Oceanogràfic, pack attire for hiking, picnics, and educational exploration.

- **Mind the Siesta Time:** Some smaller shops and attractions may close in the early afternoon, so plan accordingly. Maybe it's time for a leisurely Spanish lunch?
- **Engage with Wildlife:** If you're an animal lover, schedule a day for both Oceanogràfic and Bioparc Valencia; it's worth the time.

Chapter 3: Culinary Delights of Valencia

"Spain, The beautiful country of wine and songs."
- Johann Wolfgang Von Goethe

Valencia's culinary scene is like a sizzling paella pan, full of unexpected delights and flavors that'll make your taste buds do the cha-cha. Forget the postcard-perfect beaches and architectural wonders; we're diving into a gastronomic adventure that's as vibrant as a flamenco dancer's dress!

You are now strolling through bustling markets, the air thick with the scent of saffron, and the sea salted by the Mediterranean breeze. Think of biting into an age-old family recipe of arroz negro (that's squid ink rice for the uninitiated) that whispers secrets of Valencian tradition.

We're not talking about simply ordering a dish from a menu. This is a wild food dance with the soul of Valencia, where you'll waltz with the oranges, tango with the turrons, and maybe even two-step with a tapa or two.

Prepare to be serenaded by sizzling pans, wooed by wine that has more character than your favorite novel, and swept off your feet by flavors that you never knew existed.

So, put on your metaphorical dancing shoes, dear reader, and let's dance through Valencia's culinary wonderland, plate by delicious plate. It's a taste sensation that promises to leave you craving an encore.

Food Markets in Valencia

Mercado Central

The first stop is the Mercado Central, an epicenter of all things delicious in Valencia. Located right in the heart of the city. This market not only offers a smorgasbord of fresh produce but is also an architectural gem, flaunting Modernista design.

Envision an amazing array of colors, textures, and aromas as you wander through aisles packed with everything from jamón serrano hanging like edible chandeliers to stalls filled with ripe, juicy oranges ready to be squeezed into the freshest juice you've ever tasted.

But hey, it's not all about food; Mercado Central is a people-watcher's paradise! Engage with the local vendors, who'll passionately share their recipes and stories, or even tips for cooking the perfect paella.

Getting there: Take Bus Lines 150, 170, 26, 27, or 62 to Xàtiva Station.
Tickets: Entry's free. Save those euros for a scrumptious snack!
Food: Treat yourself to fresh horchata or a tasty empanada.
Best time to visit: Early morning to catch the best fresh produce.

Mercado de Ruzafa

Now, allow me to whisk you away to the eclectic neighborhood of Ruzafa, where the Mercado de Ruzafa awaits. This market's a bit more under-the-radar, but don't let that fool you; it's a treasure trove of culinary wonders.

Stroll through the narrow aisles, and you'll discover an array of seafood so fresh, it might just leap into your shopping basket! From marinated olives that'll make you feel like you've been kissed by the

Mediterranean sun to handmade cheeses that'll have you shouting "más, por favor!"

Mercado de Ruzafa has that local vibe, where you can rub elbows with Valencia's culinary enthusiasts and enjoy the symphony of Spanish chatter.

Getting there: Bus Lines 63 or 93 will drop you close to the market.
Tickets: Free. More money for tapas!
Food: Grab a freshly-made bocadillo for an on-the-go delight.
Best time to visit: Mid-morning for a local vibe, minus the crowds.

Mercado de Colón

Hold onto your taste buds, because the Mercado de Colón is about to take them for a ride! Situated in an astonishing Modernist building that's worth a visit in its own right, this market is the epitome of elegance. Imagine dining inside a work of art!

Here, gourmet delights meet chic cafés and stylish bars. Whether you're in the mood for freshly caught oysters or a smooth cup of local coffee, Mercado de Colón serves it with a dash of sophistication.

Getting there: Hop on Bus Line 25 or 26 to Alameda Station.
Tickets: Free. Spend on some artisan chocolates instead.
Food: Try a gourmet tapa with a local craft beer.
Best time to visit: Afternoon. Perfect for a relaxed lunch or early dinner.

Mercado de Mossén Sorell

Next, let's meander down to the Mercado de Mossén Sorell. Nestled in the heart of the charming Carmen district, this market may be smaller, but it's brimming with personality.

From organic vegetables grown with love to handmade crafts, this market is the ideal spot to fill your shopping basket with local treasures. If you want to dive into Valencia's soul, this is the place to plunge!

Getting there: Bus Line 115 to Plaza de la Reina is your ride.
Tickets: Free. Save for a locally-made souvenir.
Food: A traditional Valencian pastry is a must here.
Best time to visit: Mid-morning when it's lively but not too crowded.

Mercado del Grau

Last, but certainly not least, is Mercado del Grau. This market might not have the fame of some others in Valencia, but what it lacks in celebrity, it compensates with charm.

This local gem offers the real-deal Valencian experience. From butcher shops that'll remind you of Grandma's Sunday roast to seafood so fresh you'd think it swam onto the counter, Mercado del Grau provides the raw, unfiltered culinary experience of Valencia.

Getting there: Bus Line 1208 to Marítim - Serrería will lead the way.
Tickets: Free. More budget for fresh fish, perhaps?
Food: Savor the olives and local cheeses.
Best time to visit: Early morning when the local chefs are shopping.

Popular Dishes

Paella Valenciana

Paella is not just a meal; it's a celebration and a culinary masterpiece. But when in Valencia, don't you dare call anything with seafood a "Paella Valenciana." Here, it's about rabbit, chicken, green beans, and butter beans, all married together in a wide, shallow pan with rice and sometimes snails.

It's cooked over an open flame, usually fueled by orange tree branches. You'll smell the smoky aroma before you even see the pan. Oh, and let's not forget the saffron, which bestows upon the dish its golden hue and delicate flavor.

Where to Find the Best Paella Valenciana?
La Matandeta: Located in Alfafar, amidst the rice fields, this place serves Paella Valenciana like a royal banquet.
Getting there: It's a short drive from Valencia's city center, and some local taxis or rideshares can get you there.

Casa Roberto: Nestled in the city itself, this restaurant is hailed as the 'Paella Temple'. The chefs here have been romancing the pans for decades, and they know how to woo your taste buds.
Getting there: A leisurely walk from Valencia's central square.

L'Establiment: Located near El Palmar, this restaurant gives you the authentic experience of dining by the Albufera lagoon, where traditional Paella Valenciana has its roots.
Getting there: You might want to grab a local taxi or use a rideshare app to explore this exquisite hideaway.

Paella Wisdom from a Local

If you truly want to blend in with the Valencians, remember these rules:

- Paella is a lunch dish. Don't even think about ordering it for dinner!
- Sundays are sacred paella days. It's when families gather around a massive pan of this golden delight.

- The crispy, caramelized bottom layer of rice (called "socarrat") is a delicacy. If you get some, consider yourself lucky!

Arroz Negro (Black Rice)

You might have thought that rice only came in white and brown, but in Valencia, we love to break the mold. Arroz Negro gets its dramatic hue from squid ink, lending the dish not only an intense color but also a rich, briny flavor that resonates with the soul of the Mediterranean Sea.

Combined with fresh squid or cuttlefish, garlic, onions, and a touch of paprika, this dish is an underwater adventure on a plate. The texture is tender yet chewy, and the taste is as deep and complex as a well-aged wine.

The black color can be a bit of a surprise at first glance. But trust me, dear friend, once you've tasted Arroz Negro, your palate will be entranced, and you'll never look at rice the same way again.

Arroz Negro is like a seaside serenade, a love letter to anyone passionate about seafood and willing to explore bold flavors. It's a dish that captures the very essence of Valencia's adventurous spirit and maritime heritage. So, if you're in town, do yourself a favor and let the Black Rice cast its spell on you.

Just don't wear white—it's a deliciously messy affair!

Where to Find the Best Arroz Negro?
Bodega Casa Montaña: One of Valencia's oldest taverns, located in the Cabanyal district, they serve Arroz Negro with a side of history. Let the flavor transport you to the past.
Getting there: Easily reachable by tram or a short taxi ride from the city center.

Restaurante La Pepica: By the sea, on the Malvarrosa Beach, this establishment brings the ocean to your table. It's no wonder that Hemingway was a fan!
Getting there: Bus line 92 or 95 will take you straight to this culinary paradise.

Casa Carmela: Also at Malvarrosa Beach, Casa Carmela has been creating Arroz Negro masterpieces since 1922. The ambiance, the aroma, the flavor - it's poetry in culinary form.
Getting there: Bus line 32 or 92, or a pleasant bike ride along the beach if you're up for it.

Fideuà

Fideuà is like paella's quirky cousin. It's made with short, thin noodles instead of rice, and is a true Valencian gem. This dish boasts a fantastic mix of seafood, usually including shrimp, squid, and monkfish, all lovingly sautéed with garlic, tomatoes, and paprika.

The noodles are first browned in a pan (some even say to the point of a light tan), and then cooked with fish stock, absorbing the briny goodness of the sea. A hint of saffron adds an exotic touch, and a dollop of alioli (garlic mayo) on the side balances the flavors with its creamy richness.

Fideuà is a hearty, joyful dish, one that's ready to party on your palate. It's less formal than its cousin paella, and maybe a tad more fun. It's the type of dish that doesn't mind if you laugh with your mouth full.

Fideuà is laughter and celebration, huddled together in a pan, eager to greet you with open arms—or should I say, open noodles?

Where to Feast on Fideuà?

Restaurant Navarro: This renowned spot in Valencia's city center has been serving mouth-watering Fideuà for generations. Don't forget to try their homemade alioli, it's the stuff of legends!

Getting there: A short stroll from Colón metro station.

La Marcelina: Steps away from the beach, La Marcelina is a place where Fideuà feels at home. With the sound of waves and the fresh sea breeze, you can't ask for a better ambiance.

Getting there: Hop on bus line 92 and take in the view.

Casa Roberto: Located in the heart of Valencia, Casa Roberto's Fideuà is a nod to tradition, a perfect blend of flavor and technique.

Getting there: It's in a prime location, so simply enjoy a leisurely walk from the city center.

Esgarraet

Esgarraet is the type of dish that has your taste buds dancing the flamenco. Composed of red peppers and salted cod, it's a dish that's deceptively simple but absolutely rich in flavor. The peppers are roasted and peeled, and the salted cod is soaked, shredded, and then mixed together with the peppers. A generous glug of high-quality olive oil and a touch of garlic complete this tapestry of tastes.

The flavors blend and mingle, creating a blend of somehow tangy, salty, and sweet, all at the same time. Esgarraet often serves as a tantalizing appetizer or a succulent side dish, perfect with a piece of crusty bread.

It's not just the flavor that steals the show, but also the texture. The fish's delicate strands intertwine with the soft, succulent peppers, creating a dish that's both tender and satisfying to the bite.

Where to Delight in Esgarraet?

Bar Pilar: A favorite among locals, Bar Pilar in the historic El Carmen district offers Esgarraet with an authentic touch.
Getting there: A scenic walk from the city center, or take metro line 1 to Ángel Guimerà station.

Restaurant Levante: If you're near Benisanó, a trip to Restaurant Levante for their Esgarraet is worth the journey. They've mastered the art of this dish.
Getting there: Car travel is most convenient, or you can catch a regional train to Benisanó.

A Guide to Tapas Bars

Tapas is Spain's glorious gift to the world of food, an excuse to savor an entire meal one bite at a time. But in Valencia, we don't just "do" tapas; we live it, we breathe it, and we certainly know how to enjoy it.

Bodega Casa Montaña:

Get ready to teleport back to the 19th century! Casa Montaña, with its vintage charm, offers barrels of wine and mountains of tapas (see what I did there?). Try the marinated anchovies; they're the talk of the town.

Getting there: Bus line 19, 92.

Bar Pilar:

In the heart of El Carmen, Bar Pilar has been doling out deliciousness for decades. The patatas bravas here? A symphony of spice and crunch.

Getting there: Stroll from the city center, or hop on train line C6 to Ángel Guimerà.

La Pilareta:

They say you haven't really visited Valencia until you've tried the mussels at La Pilareta. Trust me, they're not wrong.

Getting there: It's a pleasant walk from the Plaza de la Reina.

Sagardi:

Fancy some Basque flavor in the heart of Valencia? Sagardi serves pintxos (Basque-style tapas) that will have you dancing a spontaneous jota.

Getting there: Head to the city center, near Plaza del Ayuntamiento. Walking is your friend here.

El Kiosko:

This isn't just a tapas bar; it's a Valencian institution. Sit outside and soak in the atmosphere as you nibble on some of the best clams in town.

Getting there: Bus lines 148, 156, 19, 448, 45, 47, 62.

Pro Tips:

- Night Owl? Some bars get livelier as the night wears on. Tapas are a marathon, not a sprint.

- Sharing is Caring: Don't be shy. Order various tapas and share them with friends. That's how we roll here.
- Talk to the Locals: Ask what's good. Your taste buds will thank you later.

Key Takeaways

- **Markets Galore:** Valencia's various markets, like Mercado Central, Mercado de Colón, and others, provide an eclectic and authentic local food shopping experience.
- **Paella Paradise:** Valencia is the home of the famous Paella Valenciana, and various twists on rice dishes are part of the city's gastronomic soul.
- **Tapas Culture:** Tapas bars are not just about food; they represent a way of socializing and enjoying life. From Bodega Casa Montaña to El Kiosko, there's a taste for every palate.
- **Diverse Dishes:** The culinary scene offers an array of flavors with dishes like Arroz Negro, Fideuà, and Esgarraet.

Action Steps

- Create a Food Itinerary: Plan your gastronomic journey and make necessary reservations, especially in popular tapas bars.
- Explore the Markets: Dedicate a morning to explore Valencia's food markets. It's a feast for the eyes and the stomach!
- Join a Cooking Class: If you love Paella Valenciana, why not learn how to make it? Look for local cooking classes.
- Go with the Flow: While planning is essential, allow some room for spontaneity. You might stumble upon a hidden gem!
- Talk to the Locals: Don't be shy; ask for recommendations. Valencia's residents know where the best bites are.
- Embrace Sharing: When ordering tapas, get a variety and share. It's the Valencian way!

Chapter 4: Getting Around Valencia – Transportation and Tips

"I have seen dawn and sunset on moors and windy hills coming in solemn beauty like slow old tunes of Spain."
- John Edward Masefield

Grab your metaphorical keys to the city, because Valencia doesn't just roll out a red carpet for its visitors, it unfurls a network of trams, buses, bikes, and more to make sure you're zipping around with the grace of a local on a scooter. You thought finding the perfect paella was an adventure? Buckle up, because navigating Valencia's streets, tracks, and pathways is a thrilling escapade all on its own!

Getting to Valencia

By Plane: Valencia's airport, known as Valencia Airport (VLC), is your gateway to the city if you're coming from the skies. Located about 8 kilometers from the city center, it connects to various European cities and beyond. Taxis, buses, and metro lines whisk you downtown, where your Valencian adventure begins.

By Train: Choo-choo your way into the heart of Valencia via its two main train stations, Estación del Norte and Joaquín Sorolla. High-speed AVE trains link Valencia with Madrid, Barcelona, and other Spanish cities, making it a scenic and efficient option. Feel like royalty as you glide into town with your windows-turned-movie-screens showcasing Spain's diverse landscape.

By Bus: If you prefer riding the roads, Valencia's central bus station hosts a myriad of national and international routes. Companies like Alsa and Avanza offer affordable ways to reach Valencia, especially if you're traveling within Spain. Just recline, relax, and relish the ever-changing view.

By Ferry: Ahoy, maritime enthusiasts! Valencia's port is one of the largest in the Mediterranean, with ferries coming in from the Balearic Islands. It's a delightful alternative for those who fancy a splash of sea-salt with their travels.

By Car: Road-tripping to Valencia? With well-connected highways like the A-3, A-7, and AP-7, driving to Valencia is a breeze (GPS recommended). But be warned, finding parking in the city might require a treasure map or, at the very least, some patience. Park-and-ride options are scattered around the city to make your life easier.

Getting Around in Valencia

Public Transport: The city's public transportation is a tapestry of trains, buses, metros, and ferries, all seamlessly weaving through Valencia's colorful streets. The EMT's route planner is your secret weapon, guiding you through the city like a local tour guide. And with the Valencia Tourist Card (VLC), you'll feel like a VIP, zipping through the city with unlimited access and savoring a smorgasbord of free or discounted experiences.

Taxis: If you're the "I want to travel in style" type, white taxis are ready to chauffeur you around the clock. They're almost as eager to pick you up as your dog when you come home from work.

Car: Driving in Valencia is like dancing - just follow the flow of the road, and you'll be fine. Whether you're renting or using your own car, remember to respect pedestrian crossings and pay attention to those tricky right turns. And yes, parking may feel like a game of musical chairs, but with both on-street options and car parks, you'll find a spot eventually.

Bicycle: Fancy a two-wheeled adventure? Valenbisi, Valencia's bike-sharing program, is calling your name! With the first 30 minutes free and numerous rental services available, exploring the city on a bike is like riding through a living postcard.

On Foot: Sometimes, the old-fashioned way is the best way. Strolling through Valencia's compact center connects you with the city's heartbeat. Wander through narrow alleys, linger in sun-dappled plazas, and let the city's magic unfold one step at a time.

Useful Contacts

- **Tourist Info Valencia:** Need directions to that hidden tapas bar? Want to discover a secret garden? Call +34 963 52 49 08, and the friendly voices on the other end will guide you like a GPS with a touch of local charm.

- **Emergency:** If you find yourself in a bind, 112 is your magic number. Consider it your SOS in a sea of paella.

- **Police:** Misplaced your wallet or spotted something suspicious? Dial 092, and Valencia's finest will leap into action faster than you can say "churros."

- **Fire Department:** Stumbled upon a fire? Call 080 and watch Valencia's brave firefighters swoop in like superheroes minus the capes.

- **Ambulance:** Twist an ankle dancing Flamenco? Ring (34) 963 677 375, and you'll be whisked off to care quicker than you can click your castanets.

- **Hospital:** For everything from a tummy ache to a medical mystery, reach out to +34 963 89 77 00. They've got doctors, nurses, and maybe even a resident wizard to make you feel better.

- **Pharmacy:** Need a midnight remedy or an afternoon aspirin? Dial +34 963 60 03 13 for a 24/7 pharmacy that's more reliable than your favorite coffee shop.

These numbers are like a Swiss Army knife for the modern traveler, ready to assist you at a moment's notice. So jot them down, save them on your phone, or tattoo them on your arm (just kidding about the tattoo part). But seriously, keep them close. They're your lifeline in Valencia, just in case life throws you a curveball between bites of delicious tapas.

Key Takeaways

- Public Transport: Valencia's public transportation is a mosaic of railways, buses, metros, and ferries, with the EMT providing a helpful route planner and ticket pricing. The metro's six lines cover most of the city.
- Taxis: Available 24/7, Valencia's white taxis are as omnipresent as the city's sun. Credit card payments are often accepted, but carrying cash is wise.
- Car Rentals & Driving: Renting a car is a breeze, and driving in Valencia follows standard European conventions. Remember the unique right-turn rule at pedestrian crossings.

- Valencia Tourist Card (VLC): This magical card grants unlimited access to public transport for 24, 48, or 72 hours, along with other perks. A must-have for any visitor!
- Parking: Both on-street parking (in blue zones) and car parks are available but can be tricky to find. Prices vary, so be mindful of rates and restrictions.
- Bicycles: Valenbisi, the city's bicycle-sharing system, and various bike rental services offer an eco-friendly way to explore.
- On Foot: Walking around Valencia is a pleasure, especially in the compact city center. Other areas are easily reached via public transport.
- Emergency Numbers: Keep a list of essential numbers, including the Tourist Info, emergency services, hospital, and 24/7 pharmacy.

Action Steps

- **Plan Your Routes:** Utilize Valencia's public transport planner to navigate the city with ease. Pre-plan some routes to popular destinations to save time.
- **Purchase a VLC Card:** If you're planning to explore the city extensively, grab a Valencia Tourist Card online or at key locations for unlimited access to public transport and other perks.
- **Save Emergency Numbers:** Store the essential emergency and service numbers in your phone or jot them down somewhere accessible. It's always good to be prepared.
- **Explore Bicycle Options:** If cycling is your thing, check out Valenbisi or other bike rental services online, and map out some bike-friendly routes.
- **Consider Walking Tours:** Valencia's walkable city center offers much to explore. Maybe plan a self-guided walking tour or two to take in the city's charm.

- **Know the Taxi Rules:** Familiarize yourself with the standard rates and procedures for taxis, so you're ready when you need a ride.
- **Parking Strategy:** If you're driving, research parking options near your accommodation or popular attractions to avoid the hunt for a spot.
- **Create a Transport Budget:** Estimate your transport costs, including public transport, taxis, bike rentals, or car hire, and plan accordingly to keep your trip on budget.

Conclusion

Valencia, with its rich history, gastronomic delights, unique architecture, and vibrant local culture, is an undiscovered gem waiting to dazzle you. Through the chapters of this guide, we've explored the heart and soul of this stunning city, offering not just a tourist's perspective but an intimate look that can only come from someone who's been there, seen it, and tasted it (yes, the paella is as good as they say!).

From the sprawling gardens of Turia to the futuristic splendor of the City of Arts and Sciences, we've painted a vivid picture of what Valencia has to offer. The vibrant markets, world-renowned dishes like Paella Valenciana and Fideuà, and the local tapas bars create a culinary tapestry that's as rich as it is varied.

We've also laid out the practicalities of getting to and around Valencia, with a detailed guide on transportation options. Whether you prefer wandering on foot, cycling through picturesque streets, or taking the well-connected public transportation, you've got the information to explore Valencia the way you want.

Now it's your turn. Pack your bags, buy that ticket, and make those reservations. Valencia isn't just a destination; it's an experience that's calling you. Taste the oranges, dance to the local music, explore the narrow alleys, and let Valencia surprise you.

If you've enjoyed this guide, your adventure doesn't have to end here. Consider learning the local language to deepen your connection with the wonderful Valencian people. Our next book, the *"European Spanish Phrase Book,"* is designed just for that purpose. Dive into it and converse with the locals, order your meals with confidence, and feel at home in Valencia.

Don't just read about Valencia. Live it. Embrace it. Make it a part of your story. And once you've discovered its secrets, share them. Write a review, share your insights, and join us in making Valencia a place more travelers can fall in love with.

Happy travels, dear adventurer! Valencia is waiting for you, and we can't wait to hear about your journey.

BOOK 4

European Spanish Phrase Book

Explore to Win

Introduction

Hola, amigo! Ever found yourself in a Spanish mercado, drooling over fresh paella but couldn't figure out how to ask for a plate? Or maybe you've tried to find the nearest bathroom, only to realize "bathroom" in Spanish is as elusive as a perfect Flamenco dance move? ¡Ay, caramba! Welcome to the land of Spanish, a language as rich and flavorful as a good sangria.

Picture this: you're in Spain, the birthplace of Cervantes and Picasso, and you're armed not only with a camera but with phrases that let you dive into the culture, rather than just skim the surface. Imagine haggling at a local market in Valencia or toasting "Salud!" with new friends in Barcelona. That's what this book offers you, a ticket to a more authentic experience.

Now, why should you trust this guide? It's not just a boring textbook; it's your Spanish-speaking friend, patiently helping you pronounce "Jamon Iberico" without sounding like you're summoning an ancient sorcerer.

Spanish isn't just a collection of rolled Rs and ñs. It's a language with deep roots, intertwined with a rich history and culture spread across 21 countries. From the romantic tunes of a Spanish guitar to the poetic verses of Lorca, learning Spanish phrases means unlocking doors to a whole new world.

You might be thinking, "I can't learn Spanish; I still struggle with English!" Trust me, amigo, I've been there. But with an open mind and a bit of enthusiasm, you'll be saying "¡Sí, puedo!" (Yes, I can!) in no time. The key is to embrace the journey. You won't become fluent overnight, but you will master enough to enhance your travel experience significantly.

What's the secret sauce? Well, it's understanding the sounds, the rhythm, and, yes, those tricky grammar rules. But don't fret; we'll make it as smooth as a Spanish wine. You'll learn the basics of pronunciation, how to construct simple sentences, and most importantly, how to ask where the nearest churro stand is.

So, why settle for a bland vacation when you can spice it up with Spanish? Imagine returning home, not only with souvenirs but with memories of genuine interactions and maybe a few new amigos.

Ready to embark on this linguistic fiesta? ¡Vamos! Turn the page and let's tango with Spanish together. You might stumble a little, but as they say in Spain, "El que mucho abarca, poco aprieta" (He who grasps at too much, loses everything). Let's focus on the essentials and let the fun begin!

Chapter 1: Basic Phrases and Greetings

"Life is a daring adventure, or nothing at all!"
-Helen Keller

Ever stumbled into a Spanish fiesta and wished you could join the locals in a cheerful "¡Hola!" but ended up sounding like a confused parrot? Fear not, intrepid traveler! Chapter 1 is here to rescue you from the dreaded 'lost-in-translation' scenario and turn you into a master of basic phrases and greetings.

Let's imagine that you are now strolling down a narrow, cobblestone street in Seville, and you're able to greet the shopkeepers with a confident "Buenos días" (Good morning) or thank the waiter with a heartfelt "Gracias" (Thank you). It's not about pretending to be a local; it's about embracing the culture and connecting with people, one "¡Hola!" at a time.

From hello to goodbye, and everything in between, this chapter is your golden ticket to the Spanish-speaking world. It's like a warm embrace from a Spanish grandmother – full of love, wisdom, and maybe a hint of garlic.

So, ready to break the ice without breaking into a sweat? Grab your dancing shoes and let's dive into the colorful world of Spanish greetings! No more awkward silences, only warm smiles, and friendly "¡Hola!"s. Let's get started, amigo!

Here's your ultimate cheat sheet to conquer the Spanish-speaking world:

Hello - Hola (OH-lah)
Good morning - Buenos días (BWEH-nohs DEE-ahs)
Good afternoon - Buenas tardes (BWEH-nahs TAR-dehs)
Good evening - Buenas noches (BWEH-nahs NOH-chehs)
Goodbye - Adiós (ah-DEE-ohs)
Please - Por favor (por fah-BOHR)
Thank you - Gracias (GRAH-syas)
You're welcome - De nada (deh NAH-dah)
Yes - Sí (SEE)
No - No (NO)
Excuse me - Perdón (pehr-DOHN)
I'm sorry - Lo siento (loh SYEHN-toh)
My name is... - Me llamo... (meh YA-mo)
What's your name? - ¿Cómo te llamas? (KOH-mo teh YA-mahs?)
How are you? - ¿Cómo estás? (KOH-mo eh-STAHs?)
I'm fine, thanks - Estoy bien, gracias (ehs-TOY byehn, GRAH-syas)
Where is the bathroom? - ¿Dónde está el baño? (DOHN-deh eh-STAH el BAH-nyo?)
I don't understand - No entiendo (noh ehn-TYEHN-doh)
Can you speak English? - ¿Hablas inglés? (AH-blahs een-GLEHS?)
How much is this? - ¿Cuánto cuesta? (KWAN-toh KWEHS-tah?)
Cheers! - ¡Salud! (sah-LOOD)
Help! - ¡Ayuda! (ah-YOO-dah)
Doctor - Médico (MEH-dee-koh)
I need... - Necesito... (neh-seh-SEE-toh)
I like it - Me gusta (meh GOOS-tah)
I love you - Te amo (teh AH-mo)
Friend - Amigo (ah-MEE-goh) / Amiga (ah-MEE-gah)
Beautiful - Bonito (boh-NEE-toh) / Bonita (boh-NEE-tah)
Today - Hoy (oy)
Tomorrow - Mañana (mah-NYAH-nah)
Yesterday - Ayer (ah-YEHR)
Now - Ahora (ah-OH-rah)
Later - Más tarde (mahs TAR-deh)

Always - Siempre (SYEHN-preh)
Never - Nunca (NOON-kah)
Sometimes - A veces (ah VEHS-ehs)
Often - A menudo (ah meh-NOO-doh)

These phrases are your golden keys to unlock an authentic experience, so practice them and get ready to impress!

Formal vs. Informal Addressing

In the world of Spanish, how you address someone is not just about manners; it's about context, relationship, and culture. So grab your matador's cape, because we're about to dance through this linguistic arena.

Informal Addressing: "Tú" vs. "Vos"

Tú (too): Used in most of Spain and Latin America, "tú" is the informal "you." It's like calling someone by their first name. Use it with friends, family, or someone younger.

Example: "¿Cómo estás, tú?" - How are you?

Vos (vos): In some parts of Latin America, particularly Argentina and Uruguay, "vos" replaces "tú." It's still informal, but hey, that's how they roll there.

Example: "¿Y vos?" - And you?
Formal Addressing: "Usted"

Usted (oos-TEHD): Now, put on your top hat because "usted" is the formal "you." Used with strangers, elders, or in a professional setting, "usted" shows respect. In Spain, it's more commonly used than in Latin America.

Example: "¿Cómo está usted?" - How are you?
Plural You: "Vosotros" vs. "Ustedes"

Vosotros/as (vos-oh-TROHS/ahs): Think of a party with friends in Spain. "Vosotros" is the informal plural "you." It's like saying "y'all."

Example: "¿Vosotros venís?" - Are you all coming?
Ustedes (oos-TEH-dehs): "Ustedes" is the formal plural "you" in Spain but serves for both formal and informal in Latin America. It's like saying "you all" or "you folks."

Example: "¿Ustedes están listos?" - Are you all ready?

Note: The choice between these pronouns often changes the verb conjugation, so it's not just about politeness; it's about grammar too.

Commonly used expressions for different times of the day

Morning:
"Buenos días" (BWEH-nos DEE-as) - Good morning.
- Use this until around noon to greet people cheerfully.
"¿Ha dormido bien?" (ah dor-MEE-doh byen?) - Did you sleep well?
- Perfect for chatting with your host or a close friend.
Afternoon:
"Buenas tardes" (BWEH-nas TAR-des) - Good afternoon.
- From noon until the evening, spread some sunshine with this greeting.
"¿Qué tal la tarde?" (keh tal lah TAR-de?) - How's your afternoon going?
- Casual and friendly, like asking, "How's it hanging?"
Evening:
"Buenas noches" (BWEH-nas NOH-ches) - Good evening / Goodnight.

- Whether you're starting the night or ending it, this phrase has you covered.

"Hasta mañana" (AHS-tah mah-NYAH-nah) - See you tomorrow.

- Saying goodbye at night? Toss this farewell gem into the mix.

Anytime:

"¿Qué pasa?" (keh PAH-sah?) - What's up?

- The casual cousin of "What's happening?" Great for friends and family.

"¡Hasta luego!" (AHS-tah loo-EH-goh) - See you later.

- From morning to midnight, this goodbye is never out of place.

Special Moments:

"¡Feliz cumpleaños!" (feh-LEES koom-pleh-AHN-yohs) - Happy birthday!

- Anytime, anywhere – if there's cake and candles, say it loud!

"¡Salud!" (sah-LOOD) - Cheers!

- Whether it's a morning toast or a midnight celebration, raise your glass with gusto.

Opening Conversations:

"Encantado/a de conocerle/conocerte" (en-can-TAH-doh/ah deh co-noh-SER-leh/teh) - Pleased to meet you.

- Formal (le) or informal (te), this phrase is a gracious start to any introduction.

"¿Cómo está/estás?" (KOH-moh es-TAH/es-TAHS?) - How are you?

- The formal (está) and informal (estás) versions to check in on someone's well-being.

"¿Puedo ayudarle/ayudarte?" (PWEH-doh ay-oo-DAR-leh/teh?) - Can I help you?

- Whether you're offering a seat or a helping hand, this is your go-to phrase.

"¡Qué gusto verte/verle!" (keh GOOS-toh vehr-teh/leh) - Nice to see you!

- Spread warmth right from the get-go with this joyful exclamation.

Closing Conversations:

"Ha sido un placer hablar con usted/ti" (ah see-DOH oon plah-SER ah-BLAR con oo-STED/tee) - It's been a pleasure talking with you.

- Graceful and appreciative, this is a classy way to say farewell.

"Hasta la próxima" (AHS-tah lah PROKS-ee-mah) - Until next time.

- A promise to reconvene, wrapped in elegance.

"¿Nos vemos pronto?" (nos VEH-mos PROHN-toh?) - Shall we see each other soon?

- Softly checking in on the next rendezvous.

"Gracias por todo" (GRAH-syas por TOH-doh) - Thanks for everything.

- A heartfelt goodbye that leaves a lasting impression.

"¡Cuídate!" (kwee-DAH-teh) - Take care! (informal)

- A warm and friendly way to part ways with a friend.

"Con permiso" (con pehr-MEE-soh) - Excuse me (when leaving)

- A polite way to exit a conversation or gathering.

Key Takeaways

- Greeting Essentials: Mastering basic greetings and polite phrases will open doors and create positive first impressions in Spanish-speaking communities.

- Formal vs. Informal Addressing: Understanding the difference between formal ("usted") and informal ("tú") forms is vital in Spanish and can change the tone of your interaction.
- Day-specific Expressions: Spanish offers various greetings for different times of the day, enriching your conversational palette.
- Polite Openings and Closings: Knowing how to open and close conversations with grace and respect can enhance your social interactions and make you a welcomed guest in any Spanish-speaking environment.

Exercises

1. Which greeting is typically used in the morning in Spanish-speaking countries?
   a) Buenas noches
   b) Buenas tardes
   c) Buenos días
   d) Hola

2. How would you formally ask someone how they are?
   a) ¿Cómo estás?
   b) ¿Qué pasa?
   c) ¿Cómo está usted?
   d) ¿Qué tal?

3. Which of the following is the informal word for "you"?
   a) Él
   b) Ella
   c) Usted
   d) Tú

4. What is the Spanish word for "Thank you"?
   a) Por favor
   b) Gracias
   c) Adiós
   d) Sí

5. Which phrase would you use to say goodbye to someone?
   a) Hola
   b) Por favor
   c) Adiós
   d) Buenas tardes

Fill in the Blanks

1. _____ is the formal word for "you" in Spanish.
2. To say "Good afternoon," you would say _____.
3. The Spanish word for "please" is _____.
4. When closing a conversation, you might say "_____."
5. If someone says "Gracias," you could reply with "_____."

True or False
1. "Buenas noches" means "Good morning."
2. The informal way to ask "How are you?" is "¿Cómo estás?"
3. "Por favor" translates to "Thank you."
4. "Hasta mañana" means "See you tomorrow."
5. In Spanish, "Sí" means "No."

Answer Key

Multiple Choice:
1. c) Buenos días
2. c) ¿Cómo está usted?
3. d) Tú
4. b) Gracias
5. c) Adiós

Fill in the Banks:
1. Usted
2. Buenas tardes
3. Por favor
4. Hasta luego
5. De nada

True or False:
1. False. It means "Good night."
2. True.
3. False. It means "Please."
4. True.
5. False. It means "Yes."

Chapter 2: Dining and Food

"With languages, you are at home anywhere."
-Edmund De Waal

Ever found yourself in a Spanish restaurant, staring at a menu, wishing you'd paid more attention in your high school Spanish class? Well, fret no more!

Chapter 2 is your culinary guide, a trusty translator that doesn't require batteries. You're about to embark on a delicious journey through Spanish dining and food phrases that'll make ordering a breeze and impress even the most seasoned waiter. Forget about awkwardly pointing at the menu or settling for "I'll have what they're having." Grab a napkin, loosen your belt, and let's dig into the rich world of Spanish cuisine without getting lost in translation!

Ordering Food And Drinks In Restaurants

Below you'll find some must-have phrases to make ordering food and drinks in Spanish restaurants an absolute breeze. Not only will you sound like a local, but you'll also get exactly what you're craving:

I'd like to see the menu, please. - Quisiera ver el menú, por favor. (kee-SEE-rah vehr ehl meh-NOO, pohr fah-VOHR)
I'll have what he/she is having. - Tomaré lo mismo que él/ella. (toh-mah-REH loh MEES-moh keh ehl/AY-yah)
I'd like to order now. - Me gustaría pedir ahora. (meh goos-tah-REE-ah peh-DEER ah-OH-rah)
I'll have a steak, medium-rare. - Tomaré un bistec, poco hecho. (toh-mah-REH oon bees-TEK, POH-koh EH-cho)

Can I have a glass of red/white wine? - ¿Puedo tomar una copa de vino tinto/blanco? (PWEH-doh toh-MAHR OO-nah KOH-pah deh VEE-noh TEEN-toh/BLAHN-koh)

A beer, please. - Una cerveza, por favor. (OO-nah sehr-VEH-sah, pohr fah-VOHR)

Is service included? - ¿El servicio está incluido? (ehl sehr-VEE-see-oh ehs-TAH een-kloo-EE-doh)

I have an allergy to nuts. - Tengo alergia a los frutos secos. (TEN-goh ah-lehr-GHEE-ah ah lohs FROO-tohs SEH-kohs)

What do you recommend? - ¿Qué me recomienda? (keh meh reh-koh-mee-EHN-dah)

I'm full, thank you. - Estoy lleno(a), gracias. (ehs-TOY YEH-noh(ah), GRAH-syas)

That was delicious! - ¡Estaba delicioso! (ehs-TAH-bah deh-lee-see-OH-soh)

Can I have some water, please? - ¿Puedo tener un poco de agua, por favor? (PWEH-doh TEH-nehr oon POH-koh deh AH-gwah, pohr fah-VOHR)

One coffee with milk, please. - Un café con leche, por favor. (oon kah-FEH kon LEH-cheh, pohr fah-VOHR)

Asking for the Bill:

Can I have the check, please? - ¿Puedo tener la cuenta, por favor? (PWEH-doh TEH-nehr lah KWEN-tah, pohr fah-VOHR)

Could you bring the check? - ¿Podría traer la cuenta? (poh-DREE-ah TRAH-ehr lah KWEN-tah)

We'd like to pay, please. - Nos gustaría pagar, por favor. (nohs goos-tah-REE-ah pah-GAHR, pohr fah-VOHR)

Separate checks, please. - Cuentas separadas, por favor. (KWEN-tahs seh-pah-RAH-dahs, pohr fah-VOHR)

Understanding Tipping Culture in Spain:

In Spain, tipping is not as customary as it might be in other countries. It's usually considered a nice gesture rather than an obligation. Here's what you should know:

Restaurants: It's common to leave small change or round up to the nearest euro. Leaving a tip of 5-10% is considered generous, especially in upscale establishments.

Bars and Cafés: Spaniards typically don't tip in bars and cafes. You may leave a small change if you feel the service was excellent.

Service Included: Check your bill to see if service is included (servicio incluido). If so, there's no need to leave an additional tip.

Tipping in Cash: Even if you pay by card, it's more common to leave the tip in cash directly with the server.

Vegetarian and Vegan:

I'm a vegetarian. - Soy vegetariano/vegetariana. (soy veh-heh-tah-ree-AH-no/veh-heh-tah-ree-AH-na)

I'm a vegan. - Soy vegano/vegana. (soy veh-GAH-no/veh-GAH-na)

Does this dish contain meat? - ¿Este plato contiene carne? (EH-steh PLAH-toh kohn-TYE-neh KAHR-neh?)

Can I have this without cheese? - ¿Puedo tener esto sin queso? (PWEH-doh TEH-nehr EH-stoh seen KEH-so?)

Allergies:

I'm allergic to nuts. - Soy alérgico/alérgica a los frutos secos. (soy ah-LEHR-hee-koh/ah-LEHR-hee-kah ah lohs FROO-tohs SEH-kohs)

I'm allergic to shellfish. - Soy alérgico/alérgica a los mariscos. (soy ah-LEHR-hee-koh/ah-LEHR-hee-kah ah lohs mah-REES-kohs)

Does this contain dairy? - ¿Esto contiene lácteos? (EH-stoh kohn-TYE-neh LAHK-tyeh-ohs?)

I can't eat gluten. - No puedo comer gluten. (noh PWEH-doh KOH-mehr GLOO-tehn)

Preferences:

I don't like spicy food. - No me gusta la comida picante. (noh meh GOOS-tah lah koh-MEE-dah pee-KAHN-teh)
Can I have this without onions? - ¿Puedo tener esto sin cebollas? (PWEH-doh TEH-nehr EH-stoh seen seh-BOH-yahs?)
I prefer this without sugar. - Prefiero esto sin azúcar. (preh-FYEHR-oh EH-stoh seen ahs-OO-kahr)

Typical Spanish Dishes and How to Pronounce Them

Paella - (pah-EH-yah) - A traditional rice dish with saffron, seafood, and various meats.
Tapas - (TAH-pahs) - A wide range of small, savory Spanish dishes.
Gazpacho - (gahs-PAH-choh) - A cold tomato soup, often garnished with vegetables.
Churros - (CHOOR-rohs) - Fried-dough pastry, often dipped in chocolate.
Tortilla Española - (tohr-TEE-yah eh-spah-NYOH-lah) - Spanish omelet with potatoes and onions.
Jamón Ibérico - (hah-MOHN ee-BEH-ree-koh) - A type of cured ham from the Iberian Peninsula.
Albóndigas - (ahl-BOHN-dee-gahs) - Spanish meatballs.
Flan - (flahn) - A creamy caramel custard dessert.
Chorizo - (choh-REE-thoh) - Spicy Spanish sausage.
Fabada Asturiana - (fah-BAH-dah ahs-too-ree-AH-nah) - A hearty bean stew from the Asturias region.
Pulpo a la Gallega - (POOL-poh ah lah gah-LEH-gah) - Galician-style octopus.
Calamares - (kah-lah-MAH-rehs) - Fried squid rings.

Sangría - (sahn-GREE-ah) - A refreshing wine punch with chopped fruit.
Croquetas - (kroh-KEH-tahs) - Breaded and fried dough filled with ham, cheese, or fish.
Escabeche - (ehs-kah-BEH-cheh) - Marinated fish or meat.

Key Takeaways

- Understanding Dining Etiquette: Knowing how to order food, ask for the bill, and tip properly is essential for a seamless dining experience in Spain.
- Navigating Special Dietary Needs: Learning the phrases for dietary preferences and allergies ensures a more enjoyable and safe dining experience.
- Familiarity with Typical Spanish Dishes: Recognizing and pronouncing typical Spanish dishes enhances the culinary experience and makes ordering in restaurants more comfortable.
- Cultural Insight into Spanish Cuisine: Embracing the wide variety of flavors and dishes that constitute Spanish cuisine offers a deeper connection to the local culture.
- Practical Application of Language: The phrases and expressions related to dining are practical and can be used daily, facilitating communication with locals.

Exercises

Multiple Choice

1. How would you ask for the bill in a Spanish restaurant?
    a) ¿Dónde está el baño?
    b) ¿Qué es esto?
    c) La cuenta, por favor
    d) Uno más, por favor

2. Which phrase indicates a vegetarian preference?
    a) Soy vegetariano/a
    b) Quiero carne
    c) Me gusta pescado
    d) Sin sal, por favor

3. Which of the following means "a table for two"?
    a) Una mesa para dos
    b) Una silla para dos
    c) Dos menús, por favor
    d) Una reserva para tres

4. What is the Spanish word for "water"?
    a) Vino
    b) Cerveza
    c) Agua
    d) Jugo

5. How would you ask if a dish is spicy?
    a) ¿Esto es dulce?
    b) ¿Esto es picante?
    c) ¿Tiene gluten?
    d) ¿Qué es esto?

Fill in the Blanks

1. _____ is how you say "I'm allergic to nuts" in Spanish.
2. To order "a coffee with milk," you would say _____.
3. The Spanish phrase for "Can I have the menu?" is _____.
4. When asking for more bread, you might say "_____."
5. If you want to say "I'd like a beer," you would say "_____."

True or False

1. "Paella" is pronounced "Pa-ee-ja."
2. "Sin gluten" means "without gluten."
3. You say "Salud" before eating a meal.
4. "Vino tinto" means "white wine."
5. "Tipping is customary in Spain."

Answer Key

Multiple Choice:

1. c) La cuenta, por favor
2. a) Soy vegetariano/a
3. a) Una mesa para dos
4. c) Agua
5. b) ¿Esto es picante?

Fill in the Blanks:

1. Soy alérgico/a a los frutos secos
2. Un café con leche
3. ¿Puedo tener el menú?
4. Más pan, por favor
5. Quisiera una cerveza

True or False:

1. False. It's pronounced "Pa-eh-ya."
2. True.
3. False. "Salud" is used as a toast when drinking.
4. False. "Vino tinto" means "red wine."
5. False. Tipping is not customary in Spain.

Chapter 3: Directions and Transportation

"If you talk to a man in a language he understands, that goes to his head. If you talk to him in his own language, that goes to his heart."
-Nelson Mandela

Navigating the streets of Spain or winding your way through its picturesque countryside, you'll be awash in enchanting sights and the sounds of a language alive with emotion.

But wait! How will you ask for directions to that hidden flamenco show? Or how will you navigate the local metro to find that must-see historical monument? Fear not, dear traveler, for Chapter 3 is your compass, steering wheel, and friendly local guide all rolled into one.

Buckle up and join us as we explore the art of directions and transportation in Spanish, ensuring that you never lose your way while savoring the flavors of Iberian adventure. Whether by foot, car, or train, the road to Spanish mastery continues here. Adelante!

Asking For and Understanding Directions

Where is...?: ¿Dónde está...? (DOHN-deh es-TAH?)
Can you help me?: ¿Puede ayudarme? (PWEH-deh ah-yoo-DAR-meh?)
I'm lost.: Estoy perdido/a. (es-TOY pehr-DEE-doh/ah)
How do I get to...?: ¿Cómo llego a...? (KOH-moh YEH-goh ah?)
Go straight.: Siga recto. (SEE-gah REK-toh)
Turn left.: Gire a la izquierda. (HEE-reh ah lah ees-KYER-dah)

Turn right.: Gire a la derecha. (HEE-reh ah lah deh-REH-chah)
At the corner.: En la esquina. (ehn lah es-KEE-nah)
At the traffic light.: En el semáforo. (ehn el seh-mah-FOH-roh)
Take the first/second/third exit.: Tome la primera/segunda/tercera salida. (TOH-meh lah pree-MEH-rah/seh-GOON-dah/tehr-SEH-rah sah-LEE-dah)
Is it far from here?: ¿Está lejos de aquí? (es-TAH LEH-hos deh ah-KEE?)
Is it close by?: ¿Está cerca? (es-TAH SEHR-kah?)
Can I walk there?: ¿Puedo ir a pie? (PWEH-doh eer ah pee-EH?)
Where is the bus station?: ¿Dónde está la estación de autobús? (DOHN-deh es-TAH lah es-tah-SYOHN deh ow-toh-BOOS?)

These phrases should provide a solid foundation for navigating the streets, asking for directions, and understanding the responses.

Phrases Related to Public Transportation

Bus
Where is the bus stop?: ¿Dónde está la parada de autobús? (DOHN-deh es-TAH lah pah-RAH-dah deh ow-toh-BOOS?)
What time is the next bus?: ¿A qué hora sale el próximo autobús? (ah KEH OH-rah SAH-leh el PROK-see-moh ow-toh-BOOS?)
Which bus goes to...?: ¿Qué autobús va a...? (keh ow-toh-BOOS vah ah...?)

Train
Where is the train station?: ¿Dónde está la estación de tren? (DOHN-deh es-TAH lah es-tah-SYOHN deh tren?)
I need a ticket to...: Necesito un billete a... (neh-seh-SEE-toh oon bee-YEH-teh ah...)
Is this the train to...?: ¿Es este el tren a...? (ehs EHS-teh el tren ah...?)

Taxi

I need a taxi.: Necesito un taxi. (neh-seh-SEE-toh oon TAHK-see)

Take me to this address.: Lléveme a esta dirección. (YEH-veh-meh ah EHS-tah dee-rehk-SYOHN)

How much does it cost to go to...?: ¿Cuánto cuesta ir a...? (KWAN-toh KWEHS-tah eer ah...?)

Metro/Subway

Where's the nearest metro station?: ¿Dónde está la estación de metro más cercana? (DOHN-deh es-TAH lah es-tah-SYOHN deh MEH-troh mahs sehr-KAH-nah?)

Which line should I take?: ¿Qué línea debo tomar? (keh LEE-neh-ah DEH-boh toh-MAHR?)

Does this train stop at...?: ¿Este tren se detiene en...? (EHS-teh tren seh deh-TYE-neh ehn...?)

General

When does the last service run?: ¿Cuándo sale el último servicio? (KWAN-doh SAH-leh el OOL-tee-moh sehr-VEE-syoh?)

Is this seat taken?: ¿Está ocupado este asiento? (es-TAH oh-koo-PAH-doh EHS-teh ah-SYEHN-toh?)

Do I need to change trains/buses?: ¿Necesito cambiar de tren/autobús? (neh-seh-SEE-toh kahm-BYAHR deh tren/ow-toh-BOOS?)

Renting a Car

I would like to rent a car.: Me gustaría alquilar un coche. (meh goos-tah-REE-ah ahl-kee-LAHR oon KOH-cheh)

For how many days?: ¿Por cuántos días? (por KWAHN-tohs DEE-ahs?)

Can I get insurance?: ¿Puedo obtener un seguro? (PWEH-doh ohb-TEH-nehr oon seh-GOO-roh?)

Automatic or manual?: ¿Automático o manual? (ow-toh-MAH-tee-koh oh mah-NOO-ahl?)

Where can I return the car?: ¿Dónde puedo devolver el coche? (DOHN-deh PWEH-doh deh-bohl-VEHR el KOH-cheh?)

Understanding Road Signs
Stop: Pare (PAH-reh)
No Parking: No estacionar (noh es-tah-syoh-NAHR)
Speed Limit: Límite de velocidad (LEE-mee-teh deh beh-loh-see-DAHD)
One Way: Sentido único (sen-TEE-doh OO-nee-koh)
Detour: Desvío (dehs-VEE-oh)

Additional Phrases
What's the fuel policy?: ¿Cuál es la política de combustible? (KWAHL es lah poh-LEE-tee-kah deh kohm-boos-TEE-bleh?)
Is there a GPS available?: ¿Hay GPS disponible? (eye JEE-PEH-ES dees-poh-NEE-bleh?)
I need a child's car seat.: Necesito una silla de niño. (neh-seh-SEE-toh OO-nah SEE-yah deh NYEE-nyoh)
How much is the deposit?: ¿Cuánto es el depósito? (KWAN-toh es el deh-POH-see-toh?)
Can I drop the car off at a different location?: ¿Puedo dejar el coche en una ubicación diferente? (PWEH-doh deh-HAHR el KOH-cheh ehn OO-nah oo-bee-kah-SYOHN dee-feh-REHN-teh?)

Travel Schedules
When does the next train/bus leave?: ¿Cuándo sale el próximo tren/autobús? (KWAHN-doh SAH-leh el PROK-see-moh tren/ow-toh-BOOS?)
What time does this flight arrive?: ¿A qué hora llega este vuelo? (ah keh OR-ah YEH-gah EHS-teh VWEH-lo?)
Is this the right platform for Madrid?: ¿Es este el andén correcto para Madrid? (ehs EHS-teh el ahn-DEHN koh-REHK-toh PAH-rah Mah-DREED?)

Ticket Prices

How much is a ticket to Barcelona?: ¿Cuánto cuesta un billete para Barcelona? (KWAHN-toh KWES-tah oon bee-YEH-teh PAH-rah Bar-seh-LOH-nah?)

Can I get a discount?: ¿Puedo obtener un descuento? (PWEH-doh ohb-TEH-nehr oon dehs-KWEN-toh?)

Do you have student/senior discounts?: ¿Hay descuentos para estudiantes/mayores? (eye dehs-KWEN-tohs PAH-rah es-too-DEE-AHN-tehs/my-OH-rehs?)

Platforms and More

Which platform does the train leave from?: ¿De qué andén sale el tren? (deh keh ahn-DEHN SAH-leh el tren?)

Where can I buy a ticket?: ¿Dónde puedo comprar un billete? (DOHN-deh PWEH-doh kohm-PRAHR oon bee-YEH-teh?)

Is this seat taken?: ¿Está ocupado este asiento? (ehs-TAH oh-koo-PAH-doh EHS-teh ah-SYEN-toh?)

Where's the taxi stand?: ¿Dónde está la parada de taxi? (DOHN-deh ehs-TAH lah pah-RAH-dah deh TAK-see?)

How long is the layover?: ¿Cuánto dura la escala? (KWAHN-toh DOO-rah lah ehs-KAH-lah?)

Can I get a map of the metro?: ¿Puedo obtener un mapa del metro? (PWEH-doh ohb-TEH-nehr oon MAH-pah del MEH-troh?)

Key Takeaways

- Understanding Directions: Learning basic directional phrases and questions can empower travelers to navigate through unfamiliar territories with ease.

- Public Transportation: Spanish phrases related to bus, train, taxi, etc., are essential for using public transportation efficiently. From knowing when the next train departs to understanding ticket prices, these phrases facilitate smooth travel.

- Car Rental and Road Signs: Knowing specific terminology for renting a car and understanding road signs is beneficial for those planning to drive. Being familiar with these expressions can minimize confusion on the roads.

- Inquiries about Travel Schedules and Platforms: Specific phrases that cover inquiries about travel schedules, ticket prices, and platforms are vital for planning trips, connecting flights, or even just getting around town. They help bridge the communication gap between the traveler and local transportation services.

Exercises

Multiple Choice

1. How would you ask for directions to the train station in Spanish?
    a) ¿Dónde está el baño?
    b) ¿Dónde está la estación de tren?
    c) ¿Cuánto cuesta el tren?
    d) ¿Tienes un mapa?

2. Which phrase would you use to ask for a taxi?
    a) Quiero un autobús
    b) Quiero un tren
    c) Quiero un taxi
    d) Quiero una bicicleta

3. How would you ask for a ticket to Madrid?
    a) Un billete para Madrid, por favor
    b) Una mesa para Madrid
    c) Un café para Madrid
    d) Un coche para Madrid

4. What is the Spanish phrase for "one-way ticket"?
    a) Vuelta completa
    b) Billete de ida
    c) Dos billetes
    d) Billete redondo

5. How would you say "stop here, please" to a bus driver?
    a) Pare aquí, por favor
    b) Siga aquí, por favor
    c) Gire aquí, por favor
    d) Vaya aquí, por favor

Fill in the Blanks

1. _____ means "Where is the bathroom?" in Spanish.
2. To ask for "the next train," you would say _____.
3. The Spanish phrase for "I would like to rent a car" is _____.
4. When asking for a timetable, you might say "_____."
5. If you want to ask "How much is the fare?" you would say "_____."

True or False

1. "Autobús" means "car."
2. "¿Cuándo sale el próximo tren?" means "When does the next train leave?"
3. "Vuelo" translates to "train."
4. "Un billete de ida y vuelta" means "a one-way ticket."
5. "Abierto" is used to describe an open road.

Answer Key

Multiple Choice:

1. b) ¿Dónde está la estación de tren?
2. c) Quiero un taxi
3. a) Un billete para Madrid, por favor
4. b) Billete de ida
5. a) Pare aquí, por favor

Fill in the Blanks:

1. ¿Dónde está el baño?
2. ¿Cuándo sale el próximo tren?
3. Me gustaría alquilar un coche
4. ¿Puede darme el horario?
5. ¿Cuánto cuesta la tarifa?

True or False:

1. False. It means "bus."
2. True.
3. False. It means "flight."
4. False. It means "a round-trip ticket."
5. True.

Chapter 4: Accommodations and Shopping

"Do you know what a foreign accent is? It's a sign of bravery."
-Amy Chua

Finding the right place to stay and navigating the shopping scene is an essential part of any travel experience. The words you choose can mean the difference between a standard room and a suite, a bargain, or a missed opportunity.

In this chapter, we delve into the essential phrases and cultural nuances you'll need for booking accommodations and engaging in retail therapy in Spain. From asking about room availability to inquiring about sales and sizes, these are the expressions that will allow you to interact confidently with hotel staff and shopkeepers.

Knowledge is power, and with the insights provided here, you will be empowered to make informed decisions, negotiate where necessary, and fully immerse yourself in the local culture.

No more fumbling with translation apps or tourist guides. By the end of this chapter, you'll be equipped with the language skills needed to enhance your travel experience in Spain, making it smooth, enjoyable, and authentically yours.

Booking a Hotel Room and Asking For Specific Accommodations

I'd like to book a room - Quisiera reservar una habitación (kee-SYEH-rah reh-sehr-VAHR oo-nah ah-bee-tah-SYOHN)

Do you have any rooms available? - ¿Tiene habitaciones disponibles? (TYEH-neh ah-bee-tah-SYOHN-es dees-poh-NEE-bless?)

I need a room for two nights - Necesito una habitación para dos noches (neh-seh-SEE-toh oo-nah ah-bee-tah-SYOHN PAH-rah dos NOH-chehs)

Single room - Habitación individual (ah-bee-tah-SYOHN een-dee-bee-DWAHL)

Double room - Habitación doble (ah-bee-tah-SYOHN DOH-bleh)

Suite - Suite (swee-teh)

With a sea view - Con vista al mar (kohn VEES-tah ahl mar)

With private bathroom - Con baño privado (kohn BAH-nyoh pree-VAH-doh)

Is breakfast included? - ¿El desayuno está incluido? (el deh-sah-YOO-noh ehs-TAH een-kloo-YEE-doh?)

Can I have a late checkout? - ¿Puedo hacer el checkout tarde? (PWEH-doh AH-sehr el CHEK-owt TAR-deh)

I need a room with WiFi - Necesito una habitación con WiFi (neh-seh-SEE-toh oo-nah ah-bee-tah-SYOHN kohn WEE-fee)

Do you allow pets? - ¿Permiten mascotas? (pehr-MEE-tehn mahs-KOH-tahs?)

Is there a gym? - ¿Hay un gimnasio? (eye oon heem-NAH-syoh?)

I'd like to cancel my reservation - Quisiera cancelar mi reservación (kee-SYEH-rah kahn-seh-LAHR mee reh-sehr-vah-SYOHN)

Where is the elevator? - ¿Dónde está el ascensor? (DON-deh ehs-TAH el ahs-sehn-SOHR?)

Do you have parking? - ¿Tienen estacionamiento? (TYEH-nehn ehs-tah-syoh-nah-MYEHN-toh?)

Shopping Phrases

How much does this cost? - ¿Cuánto cuesta esto? (KWAHN-toh KWEHS-tah EHS-toh?)

I'm looking for a souvenir - Estoy buscando un recuerdo (ehs-TOY boo-SKAHN-doh oon reh-KWEHR-doh)

Do you have this in another size? - ¿Tiene esto en otra talla? (TYEH-neh EHS-toh ehn OH-trah TAH-yah?)

Can I try this on? - ¿Puedo probármelo? (PWEH-doh proh-BAHR-meh-loh?)

Where are the fitting rooms? - ¿Dónde están los probadores? (DON-deh ehs-TAHN lohs proh-bah-DOH-rehs?)

I'll take this - Me llevo esto (meh YEH-voh EHS-toh)

Do you accept credit cards? - ¿Aceptan tarjetas de crédito? (ah-sehp-TAHN tar-HEH-tahs deh KREH-dee-toh?)

I need a gift - Necesito un regalo (neh-seh-SEE-toh oon reh-GAH-loh)

Do you have a sale? - ¿Tienen una oferta? (TYEH-nehn OO-nah oh-FEHR-tah?)

I'm just looking, thank you - Solo estoy mirando, gracias (SOH-loh ehs-TOY mee-RAHN-doh, GRAH-syahs)

Where can I find souvenirs? - ¿Dónde puedo encontrar recuerdos? (DON-deh PWEH-doh ehn-kohn-TRAHR reh-KWEHR-dohs?)

Can you wrap this as a gift? - ¿Puede envolverlo como un regalo? (PWEH-deh ehn-vohl-VEHR-loh KOH-moh oon reh-GAH-loh?)

Do you have this in another color? - ¿Tiene esto en otro color? (TYEH-neh EHS-toh ehn OH-troh koh-LOHR?)

Is this handmade? - ¿Esto es hecho a mano? (EHS-toh ehs ECH-oh ah MAH-noh?)

Can I return or exchange this? - ¿Puedo devolver o cambiar esto? (PWEH-doh deh-vohl-VEHR oh kahm-BYAHR EHS-toh?)

Bargaining and Understanding Currency

Bargaining Phrases:

Is there a discount? - ¿Hay un descuento? (eye oon dehs-KWEN-toh?)

Can you give me a better price? - ¿Puede darme un mejor precio? (PWEH-deh DAR-meh oon MEH-hor PREH-syoh?)

It's too expensive - Es demasiado caro (ehs deh-mah-SYAH-doh KAHR-oh)

I can pay... - Puedo pagar... (PWEH-doh pah-GAHR...)

What's the lowest price you can offer? - ¿Cuál es el precio más bajo que puede ofrecer? (kwal ehs el PREH-syoh mahs BAH-hoh keh PWEH-deh oh-freh-SEHR?)

I will take it for... - Lo tomaré por... (loh toh-mah-REH pohr...)

Understanding Currency:

What is the exchange rate? - ¿Cuál es la tasa de cambio? (KWAL ehs lah TAH-sah deh KAHM-byoh?)

Where can I exchange money? - ¿Dónde puedo cambiar dinero? (DON-deh PWEH-doh kahm-BYAHR dee-NEH-roh?)

Can I pay in euros/dollars? - ¿Puedo pagar en euros/dólares? (PWEH-doh pah-GAHR ehn EH-oo-rohs/DOH-lah-rehs?)

How much is this in euros/dollars? - ¿Cuánto es esto en euros/dólares? (KWAN-toh ehs EHS-toh ehn EH-oo-rohs/DOH-lah-rehs?)

Do you accept foreign currency? - ¿Acepta moneda extranjera? (ah-SEHP-tah moh-NEH-dah ehs-trahn-HEH-rah?)

Is there a fee for using a credit card? - ¿Hay alguna tarifa por usar una tarjeta de crédito? (eye ahl-GOO-nah tah-REE-fah pohr oo-SAHR OO-nah tar-HEH-tah deh KREH-dee-toh?)

Asking For Help and Information

In Stores:

Excuse me, can you help me? - Perdón, ¿puede ayudarme? (pehr-DOHN, PWEH-deh ah-yoo-DAR-meh?)

Where can I find...? - ¿Dónde puedo encontrar...? (DON-deh PWEH-doh ehn-kohn-TRAHR...?)

Do you have this in another size/color? - ¿Tiene esto en otra talla/color? (TYEH-neh EHS-toh ehn OH-trah TAHL-lah/koh-LOHR?)

Can I try this on? - ¿Puedo probármelo? (PWEH-doh proh-BAR-meh-loh?)

How much does this cost? - ¿Cuánto cuesta esto? (KWAN-toh KWEHS-tah EHS-toh?)

Where is the fitting room? - ¿Dónde está el probador? (DON-deh ehs-TAH el proh-bah-DOHR?)

In Hotels:

Can I have my room cleaned? - ¿Puedo tener mi habitación limpia? (PWEH-doh TEH-nehr mee ah-bee-tah-SYOHN LEEM-pee-ah?)

Can you call a taxi for me? - ¿Puede llamarme un taxi? (PWEH-deh yah-MAR-meh oon TAHK-see?)

What time is breakfast served? - ¿A qué hora se sirve el desayuno? (ah keh OH-rah seh SEER-veh el deh-sah-YOO-noh?)

Can I have a late checkout? - ¿Puedo tener una salida tarde? (PWEH-doh TEH-nehr OO-nah SAH-lee-dah TAR-deh?)

Is there Wi-Fi in the room? - ¿Hay Wi-Fi en la habitación? (eye WEE-fee ehn lah ah-bee-tah-SYOHN?)

I have a reservation under the name... - Tengo una reserva bajo el nombre... (TEHN-goh OO-nah reh-SEHR-vah BAH-hoh el NOM-breh...)

Key Takeaways

- **Understanding Hotel Terms:** Knowing how to book a room, ask for specific accommodations, or inquire about amenities like Wi-Fi is crucial for a comfortable stay.

Familiarizing yourself with these terms can help ensure that your hotel experience is as enjoyable and convenient as possible.

- **Navigating Shopping Environments:** Whether you're looking for clothes, souvenirs, or other goods, understanding basic shopping phrases allows you to interact with sales staff, find what you need, and ask important questions like sizes, colors, or prices.

- **Bargaining and Currency:** Being aware of phrases that allow you to negotiate prices and understand currency can save money and add to the excitement of shopping in local markets. This skill can be both fun and financially beneficial.

- **Asking for Assistance:** The ability to politely ask for help or information in stores and hotels is not only a sign of respect for the local culture, but it can also greatly enhance your overall experience.

Exercises

Multiple Choice

1. How would you ask for a room with two beds in Spanish?
   a) Quiero una habitación con baño
   b) Quiero una habitación con dos camas
   c) Quiero una habitación con ventana
   d) Quiero una habitación con televisión

2. Which phrase would you use to ask for a discount in a shop?
   a) ¿Hay una rebaja?
   b) ¿Tienes una bolsa?
   c) ¿Tienes una talla más grande?
   d) ¿Dónde está la salida?

3. How would you ask if a hotel has free Wi-Fi?
   a) ¿Hay Wi-Fi gratis?
   b) ¿Hay una piscina?
   c) ¿Hay desayuno gratis?
   d) ¿Hay aire acondicionado?

4. What is the Spanish phrase for "Can I try this on?"
   a) ¿Puedo probar esto?
   b) ¿Puedo comprar esto?
   c) ¿Puedo llevar esto?
   d) ¿Puedo cambiar esto?

5. How would you ask for the price of something?
   a) ¿Cómo está esto?
   b) ¿Cuánto cuesta esto?
   c) ¿Dónde está esto?
   d) ¿Qué es esto?

Fill in the Blanks

1. _____ means "Do you accept credit cards?" in Spanish.
2. To ask for "a room with a view," you would say _____.
3. The Spanish phrase for "I'm looking for a souvenir" is _____.
4. When bargaining, you might say "_____."
5. If you want to ask "Is this made of wool?" you would say "_____."

True or False

1. "Tarjeta de crédito" means "credit card."
2. "¿Tiene una habitación disponible?" Means "Do you have a room available?"
3. "Cerrado" translates to "open."
4. "Rebaja" means "return."
5. "Talla" is used to describe the size of clothing.

Answer Key

Multiple Choice:

1. b) Quiero una habitación con dos camas
2. a) ¿Hay una rebaja?
3. a) ¿Hay Wi-Fi gratis?
4. a) ¿Puedo probar esto?
5. b) ¿Cuánto cuesta esto?

Fill in the Blanks:

1. ¿Aceptan tarjetas de crédito?
2. Quiero una habitación con vista
3. Busco un recuerdo
4. ¿Puede darme un descuento?
5. ¿Esto es de lana?

True or False:

1. True.
2. True.
3. False. It means "closed."
4. False. It means "discount."
5. True.

Chapter 5: Health, Safety, and Emergency Situations

"Learning another language is not only learning different words for the same things, but learning another way to think about things."
-Flora Lewis

Welcome to Chapter 5, where we tackle the Spanish phrases that you hope you'll never have to use but really should know—just in case! Ever found yourself needing to ask for a band-aid but ended up with a baguette? Or perhaps you tried to inquire about allergies and ended up adopting an alpaca?

Fear not! This chapter will arm you with the essential phrases for health, safety, and those 'I-can't-believe-this-is-happening' moments. From visiting a doctor to reporting a stolen wallet, we'll make sure you're prepared for anything—except maybe that alpaca situation. You're on your own with that one.

Medical Emergencies

Call an ambulance! - ¡Llame a una ambulancia! (YAH-may ah OO-na am-boo-LAHN-see-ah)

I need a doctor! - ¡Necesito un médico! (neh-seh-SEE-toh oon MEH-dee-koh)

I'm injured! - ¡Estoy herido! (es-TOY eh-REE-doh) / ¡Estoy herida! (for females) (es-TOY eh-REE-dah)

It's an emergency! - ¡Es una emergencia! (es OO-na eh-mehr-HEN-see-ah)

Doctor Appointments

I have an appointment - Tengo una cita (TEHN-goh OO-na SEE-tah)
I feel sick - Me siento mal (meh SYEN-toh mahl)
What's the diagnosis? - ¿Cuál es el diagnóstico? (kwahl es el dee-ahg-NO-stee-koh)
Is it serious? - ¿Es grave? (es GRAH-veh)
I need a prescription - Necesito una receta (neh-seh-SEE-toh OO-na reh-KEH-tah)

Pharmacies

Where is the pharmacy? - ¿Dónde está la farmacia? (DON-deh es-TAH lah far-MAH-see-ah)
I need this medication - Necesito este medicamento (neh-seh-SEE-toh ES-teh meh-dee-kah-MEHN-toh)
Is this over-the-counter? - ¿Esto es sin receta? (ES-toh es seen reh-KEH-tah)
What are the side effects? - ¿Cuáles son los efectos secundarios? (KWAH-lehs son lohs eh-FEHK-tohs seh-koon-dar-ee-ohs)
How much does it cost? - ¿Cuánto cuesta? (KWAN-toh KWEH-stah)

Expressing Pain

It hurts here - Me duele aquí (meh DWEH-leh ah-KEE)
I have a headache - Tengo dolor de cabeza (TEHN-goh doh-LOHR deh ka-BEH-sah)
I've twisted my ankle - Me he torcido el tobillo (meh eh tor-THEE-doh el toh-BEE-yoh)
My stomach hurts - Me duele el estómago (meh DWEH-leh el es-TOH-mah-goh)
I have a toothache - Tengo dolor de muela (TEHN-goh doh-LOHR deh mweh-LAH)

Describing Illness

I feel nauseous - Me siento mareado/a (meh SYEN-toh mah-reh-AH-doh/dah)
I have a fever - Tengo fiebre (TEHN-goh FEE-eh-breh)

I have a cold - Tengo un resfriado (TEHN-goh oon rehs-free-AH-doh)
I'm allergic to... - Soy alérgico/a a... (soy al-EHR-hee-koh/ah ah...)
I have a rash - Tengo una erupción (TEHN-goh OO-nah eh-roop-see-OHN)

Asking for Specific Medical Assistance
Can you take my temperature? - ¿Puede tomar mi temperatura? (PWEH-deh toh-MAHR mee tehm-peh-ra-TOO-rah)
I need an X-ray - Necesito una radiografía (neh-seh-SEE-toh OO-nah rah-dee-oh-GRAH-fee-ah)
Do I need surgery? - ¿Necesito una cirugía? (neh-seh-SEE-toh OO-nah seer-OO-hee-ah)
Can I get a vaccination? - ¿Puedo recibir una vacuna? (PWEH-doh reh-see-BEER OO-nah vah-KOO-nah)
I need a blood test - Necesito un análisis de sangre (neh-seh-SEE-toh oon ah-NAH-lee-sees deh SAHN-greh)

Reporting Theft
I've been robbed - Me han robado (meh ahn roh-BAH-doh)
My purse/wallet was stolen - Me han robado la cartera (meh ahn roh-BAH-doh lah kahr-TEH-rah)
My car has been stolen - Me han robado el coche (meh ahn roh-BAH-doh el KOH-cheh)
Call the police! - ¡Llame a la policía! (YA-meh ah lah poh-lee-SEE-ah)
I need to report a theft - Necesito denunciar un robo (neh-seh-SEE-toh deh-noon-SYAR oon ROH-boh)

Reporting Lost Items
I've lost my passport - He perdido mi pasaporte (eh PEHR-dee-doh mee pah-sah-POHR-teh)
I can't find my phone - No encuentro mi teléfono (noh en-KWEN-troh mee teh-LEH-foh-noh)
I lost my luggage - Perdí mi equipaje (PEHR-dee mee eh-kee-PAH-heh)

I've lost my keys - He perdido mis llaves (eh PEHR-dee-doh mees YA-vays)
Can you help me find...? - ¿Puede ayudarme a encontrar...? (PWEH-deh ah-yoo-DAR-meh ah en-kohn-TRAHR...?)

Interacting with the Police
Here's my identification - Aquí tiene mi identificación (ah-KEE TYEH-neh mee ee-den-tee-fee-kah-see-OHN)
Where is the police station? - ¿Dónde está la comisaría? (DOHN-deh es-TAH lah koh-mee-sah-REE-ah)
Can I speak to someone who speaks English? - ¿Puedo hablar con alguien que hable inglés? (PWEH-doh ah-BLAHR kohn ahl-GYEHN keh AH-bleh een-GLEHS?)
I want to file a report - Quiero poner una denuncia (KYEH-roh poh-NEHR OO-nah deh-noon-SYAH)

Emergency Phone Numbers in Spain
General Emergency (Police, Fire, Medical): 112 (available in multiple languages, including English)
National Police: 091
Local Police: 092
Fire Brigade: 080
Medical Emergency (Ambulance): 061

How to Call for Help
Dial the appropriate number for your emergency. If you're unsure, dial the general emergency number 112, as operators can direct your call to the right service.
Stay calm and clear. Explain the situation succinctly.
Provide your location. Make sure to provide specific details, including street name and any nearby landmarks.
Wait for instructions. The operator may ask additional questions and provide instructions; follow them closely.

Helpful Phrases
I need an ambulance - Necesito una ambulancia (neh-seh-SEE-toh OO-nah ahm-boo-LAHN-syah)
There's a fire - Hay un incendio (eye oon een-SEN-dee-oh)
I need the police - Necesito la policía (neh-seh-SEE-toh lah poh-lee-SEE-ah)
I've had an accident - He tenido un accidente (eh teh-NEE-doh oon ahk-see-DEHN-teh)
I'm at [location] - Estoy en [location] (ehs-TOY ehn [location])

It's always good to have these numbers saved or written down when traveling in Spain. Additionally, local hotels or hosts may provide specific numbers or advice for their area.

Key Takeaways

- Medical Phrases: Knowing how to articulate your medical needs, schedule appointments, and interact with pharmacists can be essential.
- Expressing Pain and Illness: Being able to describe specific symptoms and ask for medical assistance will facilitate quicker, more accurate help.
- Reporting Theft or Lost Items: Understanding the process and having the vocabulary to report theft or lost items to the police can minimize stress and impact in unfortunate circumstances.
- Emergency Phone Numbers: Familiarize yourself with Spain's specific emergency numbers for general emergencies (112), police (091), fire (080), and medical (061).
- Calling for Help: Learn key phrases for different emergencies, from requesting an ambulance to reporting a fire. Always stay calm, explain the situation, and provide your exact location.

Exercises

Multiple Choice

1. How would you ask for a doctor in Spanish?
   a) ¿Dónde está la farmacia?
   b) ¿Dónde está el médico?
   c) ¿Dónde está la policía?
   d) ¿Dónde está el hospital?

2. What would you say if you needed a painkiller?
   a) Necesito un antibiótico
   b) Necesito una aspirina
   c) Necesito una venda
   d) Necesito un bisturí

3. How would you report a stolen wallet?
   a) Mi maleta ha sido robada
   b) Mi cartera ha sido robada
   c) Mi coche ha sido robado
   d) Mi teléfono ha sido robado

4. What's the general emergency number in Spain?
   a) 101
   b) 112
   c) 080
   d) 061

5. How would you express that you're feeling sick?
   a) Me siento triste
   b) Me siento cansado
   c) Me siento enfermo
   d) Me siento Feliz

Fill in the Blanks

1. To call for an ambulance, you would dial _____.
2. If you want to say "I've lost my passport," you would say _____.
3. _____ is the Spanish phrase for "I need a pharmacist."
4. If you have a headache, you might say "_____."
5. To report a fire, you would call _____.

True or False

1. "Tengo una fiebre" means "I have a cold."
2. To ask for a pharmacy, you would say "¿Dónde está la farmacia?"
3. "He perdido mi maleta" means "I've lost my wallet."
4. In Spain, calling 091 will connect you to the fire department.
5. "Estoy herido" means "I am injured."

Answer Key

Multiple Choice:

1. b) ¿Dónde está el médico?
2. b) Necesito una aspirina
3. b) Mi cartera ha sido robada
4. b) 112
5. c) Me siento enfermo

Fill in the Blanks:

1. 061
2. He perdido mi pasaporte
3. Necesito un farmacéutico
4. Tengo dolor de cabeza
5. 080

True or False:

1. False. It means "I have a fever."
2. True.
3. False. It means "I've lost my suitcase."
4. False. It will connect you to the police.
5. True.

Conclusion

As the pages of this book close, the doors to an exciting, linguistically rich adventure to Spain swing wide open. We have traversed a path filled with the melody of Spanish phrases, dancing through dialogues of directions, accommodations, shopping, health, and even emergency situations.

Understanding basic Spanish doesn't merely smooth out logistical wrinkles; it enriches the very fabric of your travel experience. Conversations become connections, and transactions transform into interactions. Whether bargaining in bustling markets, asking for directions, or simply ordering a cup of café con leche, your engagement with the Spanish language adds depth and color to every experience.

But don't stop here! Let the learning continue:

- **Engage with Locals:** Don't shy away from striking up a conversation with locals. Each dialogue will leave you with a lesson no classroom can offer.

- **Immerse Yourself:** Watch Spanish TV, read local newspapers, and listen to Spanish songs. Surround yourself with the language, and it will seep into your subconscious.

- **Contribute to the Learning Community:** Share your experiences, write reviews, and engage with fellow learners online. Your stories may inspire the next adventurer.

Your adventure with Spanish has only just begun. Embrace the slips and stumbles as much as the victories; they are all stepping stones in your journey.

Now, it's your turn to go forth and apply what you've learned. Your exploration of Spain awaits, beckoning you with its rich history, vibrant culture, and warm people. Unpack these phrases, use them as your guide, and find the stories only you can tell.

Buen viaje! Happy travels, and may your trip to Spain be as exciting and enriching as the language itself. Your road to fluency starts now, and it's a path filled with surprises and joy at every turn.

Adiós, amigos! May the Spanish words that have danced across these pages waltz with you through the beautiful streets of Spain.

Made in the USA
Las Vegas, NV
12 January 2024

84221600R00115